Landmarks in Digital Computing

Peggy A. Kidwell

Paul E. Ceruzzi

Smithsonian Institution Press

Washington

London

A Smithsonian Pictorial History

Designer: Alan Carter
Editor: Nancy P. Dutro

Cover: Counterclockwise, starting from the upper right corner, are details from figures reproduced in full on pages 16, 31, 65, 69, 74, and 113.

LIBRARY OF CONGRESS CATALOGING-IN-PUBLICATION DATA
Kidwell, Peggy Aldrich.
Landmarks in digital computing: A Smithsonian pictorial history /
Peggy Aldrich Kidwell and Paul E. Ceruzzi
p. cm.
Includes bibliographical references and index.
ISBN 1-56098-311-6. Electronic digital computers—History.
I. Ceruzzi, Paul E. II. Smithsonian Institution. III. Title.
QA76.5.K47 1994
681'. 14'0973—dc20
93-25428
CIP

British Library Cataloging-in-Publication Data is available.

Many of the designations of products mentioned in this book are registered as trademarks. Where the authors were aware of a trademark claim, the designations have been printed in capital letters or initial capitals.

For permission to reproduce illustrations appearing in this book, please correspond directly with the owners of the works as listed in the individual captions. The Smithsonian Institution Press does not retain reproduction rights for these illustrations individually, or maintain a file of addresses for photo sources. Photos available from the Smithsonian Office of Printing and Photographic Services are listed in the back of the book.

∞ The paper used in this publication meets the minimum requirements of the American National Standard for Permanence of Paper for Printed Library Materials Z39.48-1984.

THIS REPRINT EDITION HAS BEEN PRODUCED USING

ON-DEMAND PRINTING TECHNOLOGY, WHICH ENABLES

PUBLISHERS TO ISSUE SMALL QUANTITIES

OF BOOKS ON AN AS-NEEDED BASIS.

Contents

Preface

As members of the staff of the Smithsonian Institution, the authors frequently receive requests for basic information about important objects in the National Collections. A few weeks in Liverpool, away from routine museum tasks, allowed one of us (P.A.K.) to begin preparing historical accounts of some of these devices. This modest project has grown into the book that follows.

The objects described here are largely from the collections and exhibits of the National Museum of American History and the National Air and Space Museum. We encourage you to visit the "Information Age" exhibit at NMAH and the "Beyond the Limits" gallery at NASM. In addition to the objects on exhibit, both museums have large reference collections. Important collections of computing devices are housed at the Science Museum in London, the Whipple Museum of the History of Science in Cambridge, the Conservatoire des Arts et Métiers in Paris, the Deutsches Museum in Munich, and the Computer Museum in Boston. For armchair travelers, we have provided a bibliography that will allow you to explore specific topics further. For those interested in obtaining pictures of objects, a list of some of the photographs available from the Smithsonian's Office of Printing and Photographic Services is included.

Authors' Acknowledgments

This project has been made possible by the people and institutions who have generously provided objects to the Smithsonian over the years. We owe an additional debt to many Smithsonian staff members, and would particularly like to thank Uta C. Merzbach, Jon Eklund, David K. Allison, Peter Liebhold, Ann Seeger, Elliot Sivowitch, and Nance L. Briscoe for help of diverse sorts. Several people outside the Smithsonian have graciously read sections of the book and made helpful comments. Here we specially thank William Aspray, William H. Skelley, Jr., Martin Campbell-Kelly, Kim Miller, James Tomayko, Michael R. Williams, and two anonymous reviewers. Many archivists have assisted in obtaining photographs. We owe an even greater debt to the Smithsonian's Office of Printing and Photographic Services, particularly Mary Ellen McCaffrey. Finally, we thank our spouses, Mark Kidwell and Diane Wendt, for their patience and encouragement, not to mention a trip to Liverpool.

The Computer and the Book

This book and all of its parts have been created using computers. The authors produced the manuscript for this book on Zenith Laptop and IBM AT personal computers using WordPerfect 5.0 and on a DELL 386-based personal computer using Nota Bene and WordPerfect 5.1 word-processing software. Thinktank software was used for the index. Throughout the work the authors exchanged drafts using IBM Profs Electronic Mail on an IBM 4300-series mainframe. Sketches for illustrations were produced on a Macintosh Plus Computer using MacPaint software. The book was edited on a WYSEpc 286 using XyWrite III software. The designer produced the layouts and type on a Macintosh IISi 17/80 using Microsoft Word 4.0 with Quark Xpress 3.2.

Introduction

From ancient times, people have used devices to assist them with calculations. Digital computing tools were a part of everyday life in Greek antiquity, Renaissance Europe, and China from at least the seventeenth century. At the end of the nineteenth century, calculating machines and cash registers became routine tools of business and science, especially in the United States and Europe. Recent improvements in electronics have increased the capability and decreased the cost of calculating instruments. With the introduction of the pocket calculator and personal computer in the 1970s and 1980s, computing devices have come to be used at all levels of American society and are available worldwide. At the same time, special-purpose computers have made it possible to guide missiles of immense destructive power and to land people on the moon.

This book describes devices of special consequence to the history of computing. The objects, selected primarily from the collections and exhibits of the Smithsonian Institution, illustrate the wide range of devices people have used over the centuries. Both relatively inexpensive instruments produced in large numbers and unique instruments highly advanced in their time are represented. This book shows only a handful of the more important objects among the hundreds of digital computing devices in the collections. These artifacts suggest the long and diverse history of digital computing, coming from different cultures and originating over a period of hundreds of years. Most were made and used in the United States, although we include important objects from elsewhere.

Several different criteria have been used to pick "landmarks." A few objects are included simply to suggest the diverse ways in which people have kept numerical records and done arithmetic. Writing numbers on paper or entering them into a calculator are by no means the only possibilities. For example, the Incas of Peru used a system of knotted strings called a quipu, while some seventeenth century Britons used a set of sticks called Napier's rods. These objects were relatively uncommon. We also have included widely used products such as the

Fingers and toes are the most fundamental digital computing device.

abacus in its various forms, printed mathematical tables, and more recent microcomputers. Still other landmarks are prototypes and pioneering machines, harbingers of things to come. For example, in 1885 Dorr E. Felt of Chicago fashioned an adding machine in a discarded macaroni box. It was the first rough version of the Comptometer, one of the most successful adding machines ever made in the U.S. The room-sized ENIAC, built at the University of Pennsylvania during World War II, was the world's first successfully operated large-scale electronic computer. Similarly, the "Green Machine," built by Thomas Osborne in 1964, was the prototype of the HP9100A, an early programmable desktop calculator.

In addition to machines intended for general calculations, the book includes a few special-purpose computing devices. These range from cash registers to the totalisator (or tote machine) to flight control computers. These objects have interesting stories in themselves. Moreover, those who built them sometimes improved technologies, developed marketing strategies, and earned money. All of these factors proved important to more general developments in digital computing.

Finally, a few landmarks with important consequences for computing were built for entirely different purposes. For instance, the Jacquard loom, invented in the early nineteenth century, had a series of punched cards which controlled the pattern woven. Punched cards would later be adopted to control computing devices. To give another example, several versions of a cipher machine called the Enigma were used by the Germans during World War II to write and read secret messages. The Allies developed a decrypting machine known as the Bombe to read these messages. Neither the Enigma nor the Bombe calculated anything. However, mathematicians associated with the design of the Bombe made important contributions to the design of electronic computers. Moreover, government cryptographic agencies soon became an important, though often disguised, market for digital computers.

The objects discussed in this book are described in roughly the order they were introduced. However, the history of technology is not one of abrupt change, with each generation dropping the devices used by its forebears. Instruments like the abacus, for example, not only survived the introduction of calculating machines but are even used in this age of the electronic calculator. We have selected some objects to suggest the enduring utility of some computing devices, as well as the long years that may pass between the first version of a machine and its appearance as a practical product. This makes for a choppy narrative in places, but a narrative that reflects the reality of history.

Analog and Digital

The computing devices described here are all digital. In other words, they handle numbers by counting discrete units. Other computing instruments are analog, representing numbers by measuring continuous quantities. Suppose, for example, that one must convert lengths in inches into lengths in centimeters. One could enter each measurement into a handheld calculator and multiply by the appropriate conversion factor. Then the numbers would be represented by a set of digits throughout the calculation—-the calculator is a digital computing device. One also could look at a ruler, marked off with scales in both centimeters and inches. Looking at the measured length in inches, one could read off the equivalent length in centimeters. Numbers here are represented by continuous quantities (lengths), and the ruler serves as an analog computing device.

Analog and digital instruments need not be computing devices. A thermometer that represents temperature by the height of a column of mercury is an analog device. For centuries, the continuous motion of the hands of a clock represented time—clocks were analog devices. In more recent years, digital clocks and watches, on which time is counted off in discrete units of hours, minutes, seconds and sometimes fractions of a second, have become common.

Analog calculating instruments range from a simple ruler to astrolabes, drawing instruments, slide rules, and integrators (devices used to find the area bounded by closed curves). In the 1920s, analog machines called differential analyzers were built to solve problems in ballistics, electric power generation, and industrial control. These machines were among the most complex, as well as the most powerful, computing tools then available.

During World War II, inventors built digital computers using electromechanical relays and then vacuum tubes. These were not as fast as contemporary analog machines. For example, analog gun directors could calculate the path of an airplane rapidly enough to guide an antiaircraft cannon. Digital computers would not be able to make such rapid calculations for a decade. However, digital computers could give more precise results than analog, were more easily adapted to solve different problems, and had less of a tendency to give unreliable results as components deteriorated with age. For all these reasons, postwar development focused on digital devices.

The introduction of digital computers did not bring an end to analog computing—architects still use drawing instruments and students graph and read curves. Although electronic analog computers are no longer generally sold, there are "hybrid" computers which combine both analog and digital parts. Nonetheless, most electronic computing devices now use digital design. Curiously, the results of digital computations may be displayed in what appears to be an analog form. For example, some electronic calculators plot graphs, and the readings of a scanning tunneling microscope are translated into computer images of whatever surface is studied. Indeed, popular computer graphics programs allow the user to "paint" what appear to be continuous images. At the same time, some programmers have devised programs to emulate historic analog instruments such as the slide rule and the astrolabe. Similarly, contemporary computer workstations often display the time of day in the form of an analog clock in the upper right hand corner of the screen. In all of these instances, however, fundamental calculations are carried out digitally and the images only *appear* to be continuous.

Computing Devices that Don't Compute— Digital Aids to Computation

Aids to computation, in the limited sense that the term is used here, do not calculate. They simply help people to record numbers and to calculate for themselves. As the term "digital" suggests, fingers and toes have long been used for this purpose, and are the most fundamental device in this category. Many other objects have also served this end.

This chapter describes five kinds of aids to computation. The first such device is a string or strings, knotted to represent one or more numbers. Perhaps the best known of these is the quipu, used by the Incas at the time of the Spanish conquest of Peru. Second, we discuss various forms of the abacus, that is to say rows of stones, metal discs, or beads used in performing arithmetic in the Middle East at the time of Christ, in the European Renaissance, and in Russia, China, and Japan to this day. A third, less widely used, instrument is a set of rods, introduced by the Scottish mathematician John Napier in 1617. Napier's rods were designed to assist in multiplication, division, and taking square and cube roots. The very existence of these devices suggests, in a tangible way, just how difficult arithmetic appeared to some seventeenth century scholars (though not, one should hasten to add, to Napier himself).

Roman numerals are far less convenient for reckoning in one's head than those used by the ancient Babylonians. If one calculates with counters, however, Roman numerals are quite convenient. They appear in European financial statements from as late as the 16th century.

During the eighteenth and nineteenth centuries, Europeans and Americans increasingly learned to add, subtract, multiply and divide in their heads, writing down the problem, intermediate results, and final answer. An apt symbol of the use of written digits as an aid to computation is the slate, which was especially popular in figuring done in school and out of doors. Hence the fourth object described is a slate. Fifth, mathematicians, scientists, businessmen and others prepared and used printed tables of the values of various functions. As published books became less expensive, such tables became more widely available.

Aids to computation pointed the way toward machines

that could actually add, subtract, multiply and divide, and not merely assist in this process. At the same time, some digital aids are still being used, both in the United States and in other parts of the world.

The Quipu

From ancient times, people who could not read or write used knotted strings to keep records. For the Hebrew people of the Bible, knots served as memory devices. Roman tax-gatherers in Palestine kept records of their receipts on knotted cords. This use of knots has also been reported in China up to about the third century B.C., in nineteenth century India, and as late as the beginning of the twentieth century in Germany. Some of the more striking records of this sort were the quipus compiled by the Incas, South American Indians who governed what today is Peru and parts of Ecuador, Chile, and Argentina.

The Incas, who were conquered by Spanish troops in the sixteenth century, were efficient rulers. However, they had no written language. According to Spanish reports, the Incas used quipus to keep accounts of taxes paid in various forms (gold or sheep, for example), to keep a census of the population, and to assist in recalling past events. The quipu had a main cord, held horizontally, to which several hanging cords were attached. Knots were tied in the hanging cords at regular intervals. The shape of the knot indicated the digit a knot represented (1, 2, 3, etc.), while its distance from the main cord indicated its place value (ones, tens, hundreds, etc.). The color of the cord might indicate the kind of person or object represented.

Several quipus found in Inca graves were brought to the United States and to Europe. The quipu shown in Figure 1 is a complex record, with several dozen strings. The hanging cords are not all tied to one main cord, but branch. The meaning of the numbers denoted is unknown.

Knotted strings were also used for keeping numerical records by Indian groups as far north as what is now British Columbia in Canada. However, these records were usually simpler than those of the Incas. Of course some Native American peoples, such as the Mayans, had written number systems. In this century, the use of knotted cords to represent numbers has virtually disappeared, with written records taking their place.

References: Ascher and Ascher (1978, 1981), Locke (1923), Williams (1985).

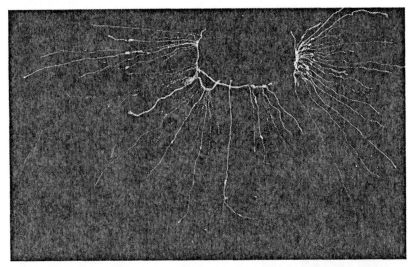

Figure 1. Quipu, with numbers represented by knotted strings. It is made from cotton and bast fibers; other quipus were made from wool. This object was found in the Nasca Valley of Peru and given to the Smithsonian in the early twentieth century. Its date is unknown. It is in the collections of the National Museum of Natural History. Photo by Rick Vargas, Smithsonian.

Counters and the Abacus

The abacus is a computing device on which arithmetic calculations are performed by sliding counters (beads, pebbles, or flat discs) along rods, wires, or lines. The instrument may have originated in the Middle East before the time of Christ. Small stones known as *calculi* (from the Greek *khalix*, pebble) were moved along lines drawn in stone or sand. Our modern terms "calculate" and "calculus" derive from the term *calculi*, while the word "abacus" comes from a Greek word meaning a board or slab, or a calculating table.

The abacus has taken many forms over the centuries. In Medieval and Renaissance Europe, merchants commonly did calculations by moving wooden or metal counters along lines drawn on a wooden table known as a counting board, a counter-board, or a reckoning-board. A man using counters (labeled with the name of the ancient Greek mathematician and philosopher Pythagorus) is shown on the right side in Figure 2. The term "counter" eventually came to refer not only to an object used in calculations but also to the place in a store where transactions are carried out. Figure 3 shows a counter made in Nuremberg in the seventeenth century.

Europeans brought counters to North America. Archeologists have found them at Jamestown and other English settlements in Virginia that date from the early 1600s. Apparently, counters were used both in trade with Native Americans and as gambling chips. At about the same time,

Figure 2. Two ways of doing arithmetic, as shown in Gregor
Reisch's *Margarita Philosophica*, published in Freiburg in 1503. Hand
reckoning is shown on the left and computation with the aid of
counters on the right. The two philosophers doing the calculations,
labeled "Boetius" and "Pytagoras," are demonstrating the relative
merits of the two methods to the figure representing arithmetic
who stands behind them. One should note that a counting table
would have been unknown to Pythagoras while the Roman Boethius
knew nothing of Arabic numerals.

the Dutch gave American Indians counters as tokens of peace. Beginning in 1738, the French shipped quantities of *jetons* (the French word for counters) to their colonies. These were intended for use by merchants and tax officials. A series of special commemorative *jetons* from the 1750s featured scenes of North America. It is not clear how much these counters actually were used in practical arithmetic, however. By the mid-1700s, hand reckoning (that is to say, calculation using written numbers) was widespread in the western world. This method is illustrated by the person on the left in Figure 2, who is labeled Boetius (after the philosopher who lived about 500 A.D.).

The counters used by European merchants were moved along lines drawn on a surface. In the Chinese, Japanese, or Russian abacus, counters move along rods or wires held in a rectangular frame. Scholars disagree about how long such instruments have been made and about whether the Asian abacus was influenced by the counters of the Greeks. Both Chinese and Japanese abaci have a crossbar. Counters above the crossbar have a value of five, while those below represent ones. In the Chinese abacus (*suan-pan*), there are two beads above the crossbar and five below. Most Japanese abaci (*soroban*) have one counter above and four below. Some Japanese instruments have five counters in the lower section. The rightmost column represents units, the next tens, the next hundreds, etc. (Of course, for numbers with digits to the right of the decimal point, the first column is for the smallest decimal term. In multiplication, some columns are used for the number being multiplied, and some for the product. In part for this reason, there are more columns on an abacus than are usually used in addition.) In any calculation, the counters that represent numbers are those moved against the crossbar.

The Russian abacus (*tchoty*) is held so that counters move sideways. It has no crossbar, and all counters in one row have the same value. Most rods have ten counters. An occasional rod has fewer, to represent fractions (see, for example, the fourth row from the bottom in Figure 6). The abacus, in its different forms, is still widely used in Russia, China, and, to a lesser degree, Japan. In the west, counters survive in a very simple form in the beads used to count prayers in the rosary.

Figure 3. Counter made in seventeenth century Nuremberg by Wolf Laufer. The reverse side has the motto: GOTTES SEGEN MACHT REICH (God's grace makes you rich). The counter is about one inch (2.5 cm) in diameter. It is in the National Numismatics Collection at the National Museum of American History. Photo courtesy of National Numismatics Collection.

References: Barnard (1916), Hudson (1979), Menninger (1969), Mitchiner (1988), Needham (1959), Pullan (1970), Yoshino (1963).

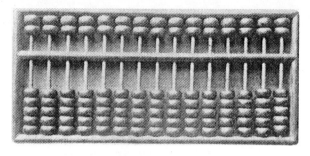

Figure 4. Chinese abacus, in which numbers are represented by wooden beads that move along bamboo rods. It measures 14⅝ × 6¼ × 1 in. (47 × 17 × 2.5 cm). It is a modern instrument that has been in the Smithsonian collections since 1928 and is now at the National Museum of American History. Photo courtesy of Smithsonian.

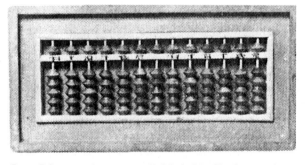

Figure 5. Japanese abacus, set in the lid of a box. The frame and beads are of wood, with bamboo rods. The bottom of the box contains writing supplies. The instrument measures 6⅝ × 3⅜ × ⅞ in. (16.8 × 8.5 × 2.2 cm). Counters on the right are labeled in units of Japanese currency; those on the left are in the units of volume used to measure rice. This abacus was used by the schoolboy S. Tetsu Tamura from 1885 to 1897, and presented by him to the American meteorologist Cleveland Abbe in 1906. National Museum of American History Collections. Photo by Brenda Gilmore, Smithsonian.

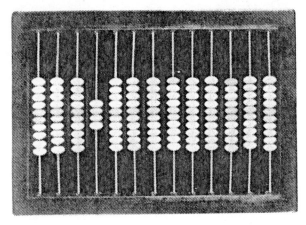

Figure 6. An inexpensive Russian abacus or *tchoty*. It is made of plastic with wire rods, and measures $5\frac{1}{2} \times 4 \times \frac{1}{2}$ in. (13.8 × 10 × 1.2 cm). It was purchased in Moscow in 1958 by the American spectroscopist William F. Meggers. National Museum of American History Collections. Photo by Rolfe Baggett, Smithsonian.

Napier's Rods

We do not know who made the first quipu or the first abacus. However, aids to computation and calculating machines made after 1600 can usually be associated with specific historical figures. Indeed, seventeenth century inventors of computing devices include the eminent mathematicians John Napier, Blaise Pascal and Gottfried Leibniz. Such a distinguished array of mathematicians and natural philosophers would not be associated with the design of computing devices again until the twentieth century, when figures such as John von Neumann, Alan Turing, and Claude Shannon turned their attention to computing.

Napier (1550–1617), a Scottish nobleman, invented a set of rods to assist in multiplying numbers and in taking square roots and cube roots. Napier's rods were generally made of wood, square in cross-section, a fraction of an inch wide, and a few inches long. Instrument makers of the day also sometimes used rods of ivory or other bone, on which numbers could be darkened to contrast with the white background. Perhaps for this reason, the rods came to be called "Napier's bones." Any face of a rod has a digit at the top and the first nine multiples of that digit in squares below. Each of these squares is divided diagonally, with the digits of the product entered from left to right on opposite sides of the diagonal. In Figure 8, the two rods lying sideways at the top give multiples of six and of four.

As with other aids to computation, Napier's rods did not actually calculate. Instead, they served as an adjustable multiplication table, used to find the partial products in multiplication problems. To multiply, say, 196 by 37, one lined up, next to one another, rods for 1, 9, and 6 (see the first three rods in the lower part of Figure 8). To find the

Figure 7. John Napier, discoverer of logarithms and one of the first people remembered as the inventor of a digital computing device. This nineteenth century drawing is after a portrait of Napier at Edinburgh University. Photo courtesy of Smithsonian.

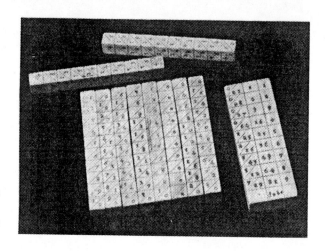

Figure 8. A set of Napier's rods. Each wooden rod is about 2¼ in. (5.6 cm) long. Ten of the rods are intended for multiplication. The wider rod on the right was used in taking square roots and cube roots. National Museum of American History Collections. Photo courtesy of Smithsonian.

product of 196 and 7, note that the seventh row is [/7] [6/3] [4/2]. Adding diagonally, one obtains the terms 7+6 = 13, 3+4 = 7 and 2, or 1372. This is the partial product of 196 and 7. Looking at the third row, one finds that the partial product of 196 and 3 is 588. But 196 × 37 = 196 × 7 + [(196 × 3) × 10] = 1372 + 5880 = 7252.

For someone with a firm knowledge of multiplication tables, Napier's rods are unnecessary. However, such standard arithmetic was not familiar to many of his contemporaries, and the rods apparently enjoyed some vogue among gentlemen of the day. Napier's account of his rods, published in Latin in the year of his death, was translated into Italian and Dutch. There even was a Chinese version of Napier's rods. Some makers produced versions of Napier's bones in which the four-faced rods were replaced by flat sticks that had numbers on only two sides. Others arranged to have all ten of the possible faces of a rod inscribed on a single cylinder. These cylinders were lined up horizontally in a box, and had thumbscrews that allowed them to be turned to the desired set of digits. This form proved impractical. Other versions of the device were produced in Europe as late as 1885, although these were not widely used. We know of no use of Napier's rods in the American colonies.

Napier had a greater influence on computation as the discoverer of logarithms. These mathematical functions were used both by people calculating by hand and as the basis of the slide rule, an important analog computing device.

References: Bryden (1992), Horsburgh (1914), Napier (1990), Needham (1959), Williams (1985).

Visitors to the United States in the early nineteenth century were impressed by how many citizens could do arithmetic. Indeed, one visitor described Americans as "a calculating people." Schoolchildren often learned to reckon by jotting down problems on a piece of slate with a slate pencil.

Students have long needed a cheap, convenient way of writing down numbers. In ancient Babylon, those who learned arithmetic wrote on clay tablets with a reed. Ancient Greeks scribbled on wax tablets. Slates were used in Europe by the 1400s. In colonial America, the relatively few children who learned to write used quill pens and paper. During the 1800s, as increasing numbers of children attended school, and as slate was mined in the U.S. rather than imported, slates were more widely used. By the 1840s, every student in a classroom might have a small slate tablet framed in wood, as well as a pencil made from slate. An 1881 advertisement for educational supplies sold by A.H. Andrews and Company of Chicago lists eight different slates that differed in size, quality, and price. The cheapest cost $2.40 and the most expensive $8.40. Although slates were sometimes advertised as "noiseless," they usually were noisy to use and didn't hold very many problems. In the second half of the nineteenth century, cheap paper became available, as did lead pencils and metal-tipped pens. Slates were gradually discarded by all but the poorest schools. They did not disappear entirely—as late as 1917 the U.S. exported some 22,682 cases of school slates (a case weighed an average of 135 pounds). All of these came from Pennsylvania. For this story, however, the slate is important as a symbol of the spread of common knowledge of arithmetic in the nineteenth century.

References: Anderson (1962), Bedini (1972), Cohen (1982), Loughlin (1918).

Figure 9. This simple slate measures 7 1/4 × 4 in. (8.5 × 10 cm). It was owned by the eighteenth century American surveyor Andrew Ellicott, the man who surveyed the site of the city of Washington, D.C., in 1791. Ellicott was assisted in this work by Benjamin Banneker, a free black farmer from Maryland who published several almanacs. National Museum of American History Collections. Photo courtesy of Smithsonian.

From antiquity, people have used tables to do arithmetic, predict astronomical events, and solve problems of trigonometry. Distinguished mathematicians and astronomers were known for their tables as well as their theories. For example, the ancient Greek astronomer Ptolemy included in his *Almagest* not only a theory of the motion of the planets, but a table of the length of chords in a circle. Centuries later, Napier not only discovered logarithms, but published tables of them. His contemporary Johannes Kepler (1572–1630), who developed an alternative to Ptolemy's description of planetary motion, also prepared tables of logarithms.

By the nineteenth century, subjects ranging from mathematical research to astronomy to insurance to engineering prompted extensive tablemaking. Even everyday business people used short, inexpensive tables to compute charges, interest, and taxes, and to convert from one form of money to another. Tables were sometimes marked on cards, rulers, and charts. They also were arranged in circles and pasted around a cylinder, with an index to allow for easy reading. A mid-nineteenth century American circular interest table is shown in Figure 10.

Figure 10. Circular interest table from 1845, designed by William B. Leavitt of New Hampshire. The outer circle of the table is labeled with amounts of money ranging from two cents to $1000. The columns of numbers below indicate the compound value of each amount, assuming interest of 6% a year, compounded annually for one to six years. The reverse side of the instrument has interest on money lent or borrowed for less than a year at the same rate. The wooden disc is 12 inches (30.3 cm) in diameter. National Museum of American History Collections. Photo by Rolfe Baggett, Smithsonian.

Figure 11. C.C. Briggs's *Useful Information for Business Men* .... This small book measures only 3 ⅓ × 2 in. (8.5 × 5 cm). Published in 1895 by a Pittsburgh manufacturer of steel, iron and nails, it sold for 50 cents and went through at least 11 editions. It includes tables of the squares, cubes, square roots and cube roots of numbers; tables of trigonometric functions like the sine and cosine, and interest tables. National Museum of American History Collections. Photo by Rick Vargas, Smithsonian.

Tables were more usually published in books, which might run to several volumes. These became increasingly common in the nineteenth century as paper became cheaper, faster printing presses were invented, and the size of the reading public grew. Some of these books, like the one shown in Figure 11, also included miscellaneous information on topics such as first aid, the apportionment of seats in the U.S. Congress, or the correction of barometer readings.

Although many of the most common tables have now been incorporated into electronic calculators and computers, taxpayers still use income tax tables, travelers sometimes have tables for converting measures and currency, and some diners use tables to compute tips.

References: Archibald (1948), Glaisher (1911), Neugebauer (1975).

Machines that Calculate or Control

Aids to computation like those described in the previous chapter have been well known and widely used. Helpful though they were, they did not do arithmetic themselves. Inventors crossed a threshold when they fashioned devices that not only represented numbers but mechanically "carried a one" when the sum of two digits exceeded nine. This ability to actually add distinguishes adding machines from aids to computation. From mechanisms that added, inventors went on to machines that subtracted (with their need to "borrow" from a column to the left), multiplied (sometimes simply by adding repeatedly), and divided.

The first adding and calculating machines were invented in Europe in the seventeenth century. They were ingenious, but not useful products. Simpler, cheaper computing methods, such as reckoning on a slate or consulting mathematical tables, prevailed for another two centuries. Only in the nineteenth century did larger markets, new designs, mass-production methods, and advances in machine tools make it possible to build calculating machines that were rugged, reliable, and relatively inexpensive. Machines were made in large quantities and diverse types. Many have been preserved, particularly in museum collections. These display a rich variety of mechanisms, sizes, and shapes.

"That this toil of pure intelligence— for such it seems to be— can possibly be performed by an unconscious machine is a proposition that is received with incredulity."
—F.A.P. Barnard, 1869, on viewing a calculating machine.

The nineteenth century also saw the development of machines that used coding to control other machines or processes. These devices originated in the medieval clocks of Central Europe, where weight-driven cams directed the ringing of bells at regular intervals. The direct descendants of these cams were drums with protruding pins that controlled a process, such as those still used in spring-driven music boxes. The details are not known, but it seems likely that someone thought to reverse the idea of the pin-studded drum, and build a device in which punched holes, rather than protruding pins, carried information. That invention led to a separate line of punched-card machines that paralleled the development of calculating machines. In the 1940s these two lines converged to give the world "computers"—machines that not only calculated, but also had a series of instructions, punched as holes in paper tape or cards, that automatically controlled the course of a calculation.

This chapter traces the early history of machines incorporating automatic control or performing calculations. We first describe a device that featured automatic control, the Jacquard loom. Second, we highlight an adding machine built in the tradition of mechanical marvels—an instrument patented by Jean Lepine in 1725. We then describe seven pioneering nineteenth century machines. Two of these, the stepped drum calculating machine of C.X. Thomas and the pinwheel calculating machine of Frank S. Baldwin, introduced mechanisms for doing arithmetic that would be widely adopted. Another, Victor Schilt's adding machine, is the oldest surviving instrument in which addition takes place by pushing keys (as opposed, for example, to turning a crank). A fourth machine, Scheutz's difference engine, is the oldest printing calculator sold. Two other objects, Dorr E. Felt's Comptometer and W.S. Burroughs's adding machine, represent the beginning of American mass production of computing devices. Finally, we include a brief section on the cash register, a machine originally built simply to record transactions over an entire day, but modified to ring up individual sales and print out receipts.

These machines are important because they demonstrated that certain human activities—calculation and the control of mechanical processes—could be carried out by machine. At the same time, the stories of these innovations suggest how difficult the process of technological change can be. The Jacquard loom faced fierce and even violent opposition from weavers before winning acceptance. Adding machines like the one invented by Lepine did not become practical products for more than 200 years. Both Thomas and Baldwin were slow to find customers. Schilt declined outright to sell adding machines, and Scheutz and his son sold only two difference engines. Both Felt and Burroughs had a rocky start in business, and the Rittys had to sell their cash register patent. Innovation does not guarantee a market, let alone financial success.

Nonetheless, innovations and/or the institutions associated with them may have an enduring influence. A few factories still have Jacquard looms. The mechanisms introduced by Lepine, by Thomas, and by Baldwin appeared in machines sold into the 1950s. Schilt's idea that addition should be performed by pushing keys is with us still. It is all too easy to assume that new technologies entirely supplant older ones; these examples suggest a more complicated story. At the same time, some business institutions established to sell calculating machines survived to make quite different products. For example, companies descended from Burroughs Corporation and the National Cash Register Company survive today as UNISYS and the NCR Division of AT&T. More generally, even when hand-operated and electrically powered machines gave way to electromechanical and electronic devices, the goals of accurate, rapid calculation and better process control endured in the minds of innovators.

Joseph Marie Jacquard and the Automatic Loom

Joseph Marie Jacquard (1752–1834), a silk weaver in the French city of Lyon, was the first person to successfully use punched cards to control a manufacturing process. Jacquard wove complex patterns in silk, patterns as complex as that shown in Figure 13. His mechanism greatly impressed the English mathematician Charles Babbage and may well have been known to the American inventor Herman Hollerith. Punched cards were used in the tabulating machines of Hollerith and others, and in pioneering twentieth century computers. Hence the use of Jacquard's invention extended well beyond the textile industry.

Weaving a complex pattern requires adjustment of the warp yarns after each throw of the shuttle. This was done

Figure 12. Jacquard loom. This loom has an eighteenth century frame and a Jacquard mechanism from the 1840s. Note the punched cards at the center top of the photograph. National Museum of American History Collections. Photo courtesy of Smithsonian Institution.

by a weaver's helper called a drawgirl (or a drawboy). During the eighteenth century, there were several attempts to find a mechanical system that would ease the work of the drawgirl or eliminate her job entirely. These involved punched paper tapes, punched cards, or a cylinder pierced with a pattern of holes determined by the design planned. None of these inventions was widely adopted.

On an 1803 visit to Paris, Jacquard found, studied, and made a copy of a loom for pattern weaving made in the eighteenth century by another Frenchman named Jacques Vaucanson. Vaucanson's loom had a cylinder indented with holes that controlled the motion of the warp yarns. This mechanism was designed to replace the work of the drawgirl, but had had little influence. Jacquard took his copy of Vaucanson's model back to Lyon and improved upon it. He designed a loom attachment in which one punched card controlled the warp yarns raised for a single row of a pattern. The cards were laced together and hung over a revolving four-sided drum. The Jacquard mechanism made it possible for a single weaver to weave complex patterns without an assistant. The woven portrait of Jacquard shown in Figure 13 suggests how detailed these patterns could be.

Figure 13. Portrait of Joseph Marie Jacquard, woven in silk on a Jacquard loom. It measures 21½ × 27½ in. (55 × 70 cm), and dates from 1839. National Museum of American History Collections. Photo courtesy of Smithsonian Institution.

Although weavers had complained about the cost of paying, housing, and feeding drawgirls, they did not necessarily relish the alternative Jacquard offered. With a Jacquard loom, the workday lengthened to 14 or 15 hours, not limited by the 12 hours that a drawgirl or drawboy worked. Weaving required less skill, threatening the wages of craftsmen. Fearing these changes, the citizens of Lyon destroyed Jacquard looms and even threatened the inventor's life. This violence abated in a few years, and thousands of Jacquard looms were built. Jacquard received many honors and awards for his invention.

Punched cards are still used to control pattern weaving today, to a limited extent. At least as late as 1990, the Pennsylvania Woven Carpet Mills in Philadelphia had thirty of these looms. They are used to produce the durable carpets needed in public places such as airports and casinos.

References: Adrosko (1982), Austrian (1982), Posselt (1988), Snow (1990).

Figure 14. Blaise Pascal. Like Napier, Pascal is remembered as a mathematician as well as an inventor. Photo courtesy of Smithsonian.

Blaise Pascal (1623–1662) was a distinguished French mathematician and philosopher. Pascal's father was a tax collector, which may have impressed him with the importance of accurate calculations. In 1642, he invented an adding machine. The work of carrying numbers, which had previously been done by hand (as with counters and the abacus) or in the head, could now be done by a falling weight linked to pegs in the wheels of a machine.[1] Over the course of his life, Pascal made about 50 adding machines. In all of these, numbers were entered by rotating wheels with a stylus. A falling weight linked to pegs on the wheels served as the carry mechanism. Although several of Pascal's machines survive, none is presently in the Smithsonian collections, and we represent him here by the portrait in Figure 14.

Figure 15. The adding machine of Jean Lepine. With the lid closed, its dimensions are 19⅜ × 10⅜ × 1⅞ in. (49.2 × 26.4 × 4.8 cm). The mechanism is brass and steel attached under a brass surface. The box holding it is wood covered with leather. National Museum of American History Collections. Photo courtesy of Smithsonian.

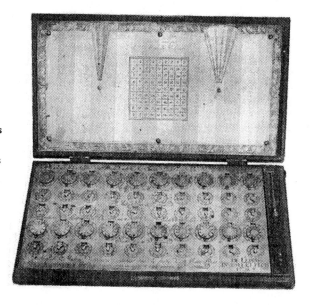

1. The German professor Wilhelm Schickard had already described an adding machine he had designed in correspondence with Johannes Kepler in 1623 and 1624. However, apparently only one example was actually completed and no description of the invention was published until the twentieth century.

Pascal's device inspired other adding machines, like the one shown in Figure 15. This was made in 1725 by Jean Lepine, watchmaker and mechanician to King Louis XV of France. In Lepine's device, carrying took place through the flex of a spring and not the fall of a weight. The first row of large circles was used for addition or, if one added repeatedly, for multiplication. Each circle represented a digit. To enter a number, one rotated the inner circle using the stylus on the right side. The sum appeared in the windows at the top of the large circles. The rows of small circles were for keeping track of numbers that had been entered. The second row of large circles was used for sub-traction. The brass plate on the inside of the lid of Lepine's machine contained a 9 × 9 multiplication table. Two rotating discs behind the plate assisted in computing mul-tiples of unit prices. Although Lepine made more than one copy of his adding machine, it never became popular. This example of Lepine's work is noteworthy not only because it is in the tradition of Pascal, but because it was owned and repaired by Charles Xavier Thomas, the inventor of the first commercially successful calculating machine.

Simpler stylus-operated adding machines would sell well in the late nineteenth and early twentieth centuries. The first of these successfully marketed in the United States was a two-wheeled adding machine, patented in 1868 by the American journalist Charles Henry Webb. It sold in various forms until the turn of the century. An early Webb adder is shown in Figure 16.

References: l'Académie royale des sciences (1735), Baillie (1982), Kidwell (1986).

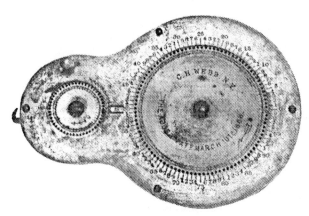

Figure 16. Webb adder. This version of Webb's adding machine measures 6¾ × 5¼ × ⅞ in. (17 × 13.3 × 2.2 cm) and is made of metal with a wooden back. National Museum of American History Collections. Photo by Jeff Plosanka, Smithsonian.

Charles Xavier Thomas (1785–1870) invented and sold the first commercially successful calculating machine. Born in the town of Colmar in eastern France, Thomas moved to Paris and helped to start the French insurance industry. He spent most of his life as the head of the Compagnie d'Assurance Le Soleil.

Thomas undoubtedly was aware of how much the insurance industry needed accurately computed tables. To assist with this work, he invented a machine he called the "arithmometer," which he patented in 1820. He also pre-

Figure 17. Charles Xavier Thomas's arithmometer of 1820, the model for the first successfully marketed calculating machine. The model is made of brass, steel and wood, and was operated by pulling a ribbon. It fits into a velvet-lined, leather-covered case, which measures (closed) 11⅝ × 5¼ × 3¼ in. (29.5 × 13.4 × 8.2 cm). Later Thomas arithmometers had a brass and steel mechanism, were operated by turning a crank, and fit into wooden cases. National Museum of American History Collections. Photo courtesy of Smithsonian.

Figure 18. The underside of the Thomas arithmometer shown in Figure 17. Note the three stepped drums on the right and the ribbon wound on a spool on the left. The teeth on each drum differ in length, giving a "stepped" appearance. Pulling the ribbon drives the machine. Photo courtesy of Smithsonian.

sented the model arithmometer shown in Figure 17 to the French Society for the Encouragement of National Industry (Société d'encouragement pour l'industrie nationale). To enter a number on the model, one pulled up a lever for each digit (in later Thomas machines, one would pull a lever down). In the photograph, the three levers on the right are set at zero. The position of the fourth lever determines whether the machine is set for addition or for sub-

Figure 19. Actuaries' office at Aetna Life Insurance Company in Hartford, Connecticut, 1890. Note the arithmometer on the left. Photo courtesy of Aetna Life and Casualty Archives.

Figure 20. The last of the stepped-drum calculating machines, the Curta. This handheld machine has a diameter of only 2½ in. (6.3 cm) and is 4¼ in. (11 cm) high. The Austrian Curt Herzstark (1902–1988) worked out the design during World War II as a prisoner in the Nazi concentration camp at Buchenwald. National Museum of American History Collections. Photo by Jeff Plosonka, Smithsonian.

traction. Underneath each of the three levers on the right is a rotating cylinder called a stepped drum. These are shown from below in Figure 18. Each cylinder has nine teeth that vary in length—if the lever is set at 9, nine teeth are engaged; at 8, eight teeth, and so forth. Rotating the stepped drums causes the numeral wheels at the back of the machine to rotate in proportion to the number entered. In this model, one pulls a ribbon to rotate the *drums (the ribbon is visible in Figure 18). In later Thomas machines, users rotated a crank. The carriage carrying the numeral wheels may be moved over, which makes it possible to multiply by tens, hundreds and thousands, not just by units. The presence of this carriage distinguished Thomas's and other calculating machines from simple adding machines.

Stepped-drum calculating machines were built as early as the 1670s by the German philosopher and mathematician Gottfried Wilhelm Leibniz. Thomas was the first to sell such machines regularly over a number of years. With the assistance of his son, he made steady improvements. They hired skilled mechanics to actually make the machines. Use of arithmometers spread gradually: some 500 machines sold between 1825 and 1865, and 1000 from 1865 to 1878. In the late nineteenth century, stepped-drum calculating machines like those of Thomas were manufactured in Germany and England as well as in France. Figure 19 shows one of these machines in use at a Hartford insurance company. Not only these machines, but calculating machines built on quite different principles, like those of W.T. Odhner and W.S. Burroughs, were often called "arithmometers."

By the mid-twentieth century, Thomas machines had been relegated to museum collections and the name arithmometer was antiquated at best. However, a small, hand-held stepped-drum calculating machine called the Curta was still manufactured in Liechtenstein and sold worldwide (see Figure 20). It was displaced only by the electronic calculators of the 1970s.

References: Anonymous (November, 1988), Beauclair (1968), Herzstark (1987), Martin (1925), Williams (1985).

During the second half of the nineteenth century, a steady stream of world's fairs offered inventors an unusual opportunity to draw attention to their latest ideas and to bring fame to themselves and their nations. Large crowds visited the fairs, and accounts of the exhibits appeared in newspapers and magazines, guidebooks, and reports of national and international committees. Calculating machines of Thomas, Scheutz, Felt, and others, as well as the tabulating machine of Herman Hollerith described in the next chapter, won considerable publicity at these international expositions.

Victor Schilt (1822–1880), a little-known clockmaker from the Swiss canton of Solothurn, sent the adding machine shown in Figure 21 to the first of the great world's fairs, the Crystal Palace Exposition held in London in 1851. This machine is the oldest extant adding machine driven directly by pushing keys. Earlier machines required a stylus to rotate wheels (as in Lepine's machine) or had numbers set with levers (as in Thomas's machine). The device added numbers up to a sum of 299. Schilt won an honorable mention at the fair. He also reportedly received an order for 100 adding machines, but refused to fill it.

Schilt was but one of several inventors who proposed key-driven machines at mid-century. Such devices would not be commercially successful until later in the century. Keys are one of the few innovations made on mechanical calculating machines that have been preserved on present-day electronic calculators.

References: d'Ocagne (1986), Turck (1921).

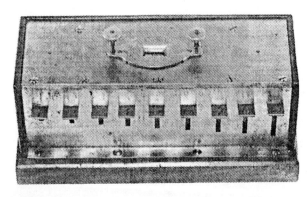

Figure 21. Victor Schilt's key-driven adding machine, exhibited in 1851. The nine keys (there is no zero key) run across the front of the machine. The machine is made of brass and steel and fits into a wooden frame. It measures 10¼ × 5¾ × 4½ in. (26 ×14.7 × 11.5 cm). National Museum of American History Collections. Photo courtesy of Smithsonian.

The Swedish publisher Georg Scheutz (1785–1873) was intrigued by literature, political reform, science, and new technology. As a publisher, he was most aware of printing errors, including those that arose in the production of mathematical tables. In 1820, the English mathematician Charles Babbage had envisioned an "engine" that would carry out such computations and print the results. He called the machine a difference engine because it calculated successive values of a function by a mathematical technique known as the method of finite differences. Babbage had constructed part of his machine by 1822, and obtained considerable funds from the British government to complete it. However, problems with finances and management prevented him from completing the task.

Inspired by Babbage's work, Georg Scheutz and his son Edvard Scheutz (1821–1881) designed a machine to calculate numerical tables and print the results on molds made out of papier mâché or soft metal. These molds then served as a pattern from which the stereotype plates used in printing were made. This avoided the usual errors introduced when numbers were set in type by a printer copying from a manuscript. In 1853, after considerable preliminary work, the Scheutzes completed the first machine they sold. It was the first operable printing calculator sold.

The Scheutz difference engine, shown in Figure 22, won a gold medal at the Paris Exposition of 1855. It was purchased by the newly established Dudley Observatory in Albany, New York, for 1000 pounds in British cur-

Figure 22. Scheutz difference engine used at the Dudley Observatory in New York. It is made of brass, steel and iron, with a wooden base and handle. It measures, overall, 67 × 22¼ × 27 in. (170 × 58 × 56 cm). The top row of wheels represents the values of a sequence of numbers, the second row shows the difference between two successive values of these numbers, the third row second differences, and so forth. National Museum of American History Collections. Photo courtesy of Smithsonian.

rency. Astronomers at the Dudley used the difference engine in computations relating the refraction of starlight and the motion of Mars. This work was partly funded by the U.S. Nautical Almanac Office, marking the beginning of the involvement of the United States government with digital computing devices. Like many later scientists, those at the Dudley Observatory were more interested in carrying out computations than in preparing them for the press. They apparently did not produce stereomolds, but were content to have results printed on paper.

A second Scheutz difference engine was made in England and used by the British government for calculations relating to life expectancy. A few other people, including the American George Grant, also tried to construct difference engines. These efforts were eclipsed when astronomers and others realized that they could carry out all the mathematical operations of a difference engine by a careful use of the simpler—and cheaper—machines such as those being produced by Burroughs Adding Machine Company, National Cash Register, and IBM. These machines were descendants of the early products of these companies described in this and the following chapter.

References: Lindgren (1987), Merzbach (1977), Walford (1871).

Frank S. Baldwin and Pinwheel Calculating Machines

In the early 1870s, a Connecticut-born inventor named Frank S. Baldwin (1838–1925) was called on to repair a Thomas arithmometer at the office of an insurance company in St. Louis. Baldwin soon envisioned and patented a smaller and lighter form of calculating machine. Instead of stepped drums, he used a set of pinwheels—gears on

Figure 23. Frank S. Baldwin's calculating machine, patented in 1875. It has a brass exterior with a wooden base and measures, overall, 7 1/2 × 8 1/2 × 6 in. (19 × 21.5 × 15 cm). The invention won a gold medal from Philadelphia's Franklin Institute in 1874, but Baldwin sold only a few copies. National Museum of American History Collections. Photo courtesy of Smithsonian.

Figure 24. An early Odhner calculating machine, made in St. Petersburg about 1890. It measures 10¹/₄ × 6¹/₂ × 5¹/₄ in. (26 ×16.3 × 13.2 cm). The machine has an iron or steel exterior, a brass mechanism, and a wooden base. Note that this machine is called an "arithmometer," although it has a pinwheel mechanism. The machine has been restored. Photo courtesy of Smithsonian.

which the number of teeth or pins may vary. All the pinwheels were mounted on one shaft. The number of pins protruding from a wheel was set by moving a lever. Once all the pinwheels were set, the shaft was rotated clockwise to add or counterclockwise to subtract. Baldwin applied for a patent in 1873 and received it in 1875. Although his invention was praised by government and railway officials, the pinwheel calculating machine invented at about the same time by W.T. Odhner, a Swede living in Russia, was sturdier and easier to read, and sold much better at first. An Odhner calculating machine used by Joseph S. McCoy, Actuary of the U.S. Treasury Department, is shown in Figure 24. Odhner-type machines, which could handle larger numbers than many stepped-drum machines, were manufactured as "Brunsvigas" in Germany and, after 1913, as "Marchants" in the United States.

In 1911, after almost 40 years of tinkering with calculating machines, Baldwin joined forces with a young New York lawyer named Jay R. Monroe. Monroe calculating machines, which incorporated Baldwin's inventions, were sturdy machines for the office. Numbers were set by pushing keys rather than setting levers, a practice that would become standard. These calculators soon had a considerable market.

References: Locke (1922, 1928), Williams (1985).

Dorr E. Felt (1862–1930) was the son of a Wisconsin politician. He apprenticed at a machine shop in that state and then, in 1882, went to work for the Pullman Company in Chicago. In 1884, Felt resolved to design an improved adding machine for accountants. Like Schilt, he was interested in key-driven machines, but he wanted customers to be able to add larger numbers and to add them quickly.

When Felt set out to make his first model, he didn't have the cash for elegance. A macaroni box from a local store provided the frame for his machine. Meat skewers served as keys, staples kept the keys in line, and rubber bands served for springs. Felt's first rough model is shown in Figure 25. He finished it in early 1885. By the end of 1887, he had named his machine the Comptometer, patented it, built eight working copies, and distributed these copies to government officials, businessmen and others who might provide useful testimonials. One of Felt's first eight machines is shown in Figure 26. Felt formed a partnership with Robert Tarrant, and the firm of Felt & Tarrant went on to sell Comptometers in the United States and abroad for over fifty years. In the 1890s, new machines cost about $125.

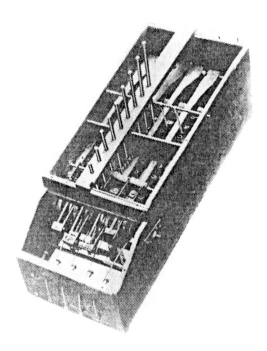

Figure 25. Dorr E. Felt's model of a Comptometer, made in a wooden macaroni box. It measures 9 × 20½ × 9⅝ in. (23 × 52 × 24.5 cm). National Museum of American History Collections. Photo courtesy of Smithsonian.

Figure 26. One of the first eight Comptometers Felt produced for regular use. It has metal keys and a wooden frame, and measures 7 ¾ × 14 ⁷/₈ × 6 ⅛ in. (19.7 × 37.8 ×15.5 cm). It was used by Joseph S. McCoy, Actuary of the United States Treasury Department. National Museum of American History Collections. Photo by Brenda Gilmore, Smithsonian.

Checking Teacher. "I just know she's wrong."

Figure 27. Illustration from a 1905 booklet on the Comptometer. National Museum of American History Collections. Photo courtesy of the Smithsonian.

As the Felt & Tarrant advertisement shown in Figure 27 suggests, adding on a Comptometer was simple, with no crank to move as with the Thomas, Baldwin, Odhner, and Burroughs machines (clearing the machine did require turning a crank). Below each column of keys was a long lever, which was linked to a numeral wheel. Depressing a key pushed down the lever below with a leverage that turned the numeral wheel in proportion to the number pushed. Subtraction, multiplication, and division were not as simple, and Comptometer operators often were trained at special schools.

Unlike Schilt, Burroughs, and Baldwin, Felt was a successful businessman who was president of Felt & Tarrant Manufacturing Company until his death in 1930. He used some of the firm's profits to acquire old calculating machines, including those of Schilt and Scheutz and an early machine on the design of Burroughs. These later were given to the Smithsonian by Victor Comptometer Corporation, a company formed in 1961 from the union of Comptometer Corporation (as Felt & Tarrant was renamed in 1957) and Victor Adding Machine Company.

References: Anonymous (1955), Darby (1968), Holman (1921), Turck (1921).

As a bank clerk in Auburn, New York, William Seward Burroughs (1857–1898) became convinced that banks needed a machine that would add figures accurately and print entries and sums. When poor health forced Burroughs to leave the bank in 1882, he resolved to invent an adding machine. He went to St. Louis, took a job in a machine shop (Burroughs apparently found this more healthful than banking), and began tinkering. By 1891, he had several patents and an adding machine sufficiently reliable for use in banks. It was sold by a firm called American Arithmometer Company, later renamed Burroughs Adding Machine Company.

To use a Burroughs adding machine, an operator first pushed down the digits on the keyboard for the number to be added. Pulling the crank forward caused the entry to print. Releasing the crank added the number to those already entered. Adding took place through a system of toothed segments and gears. In the early machine shown, the only way to see the sum was to print it out. On later Burroughs machines, a row of numeral dials displayed the running total.

Figure 28 shows an example of the first model sold by the American Arithmometer Company. It was introduced in 1890, but did not work well and was withdrawn the following year. Despite this early setback, Burroughs persevered, and soon had a successful product. By 1926,

Figure 28. An 1890 adding machine by the American Arithmometer Company, built on the design of W.S. Burroughs. It measures 11 ×15 ×12.5 in. (28 × 38 × 32 cm). Reading the paper tape at the back of the machine was the only way to find the result. National Museum of American History Collections. Photo courtesy of Smithsonian.

Burroughs Adding Machine Company had sold over a million machines. These came in a wide variety of styles. By 1909, they ranged in price from $175 to $575, with possible additional charges for special features. Unfortunately for Burroughs, ill health plagued him in the 1890s, he was forced to retire in 1897, and he died the next year. Burroughs Adding Machine Company (after 1953, Burroughs Corporation) remained an active manufacturer of calculating machines and then computers. In the 1980s it merged with Sperry Univac to form Unisys.

References: Anonymous (1939), Horsburgh (1914), d'Ocagne (1986).

The Ritty Cash Register

Not all nineteenth century innovations in computing were adding and calculating machines. As American business expanded in the second half of the century, and cash transactions superseded barter as a basis for exchanging goods, merchants took various steps to secure their money. The use of safes and locked cash drawers provided some defense against intruders. It was more difficult to prevent clerks from keeping some of the money they received.

On an 1878 voyage across the Atlantic, James Ritty of Dayton, Ohio, reportedly was much impressed by a device in the ship's engine room that kept count of the number of revolutions of the propellor shaft. If one could mechanically count the number of times a wheel turned, Ritty thought it might also be possible to mechanically count cash as it was received in a store.

When Ritty returned to Dayton, he and his brother John, a skilled mechanic, began working on the machine they would call a cash register. Figure 29 shows an early reproduction of their first model. Its face resembled a large clock, with one hand indicating dollars and the other cents. Two rows of keys in the front of the instrument were pushed to record sales. The machine recorded multiples of five from 5 to 95 cents and amounts from $1 to $9. Inside the cash register was a mechanism that kept track of total sales. The register was kept locked so that only the owner could see this record.

The Rittys patented an improved form of this cash register in 1879. They continued to tinker with the machine, replacing the clocklike dial with "pop-up" numbers that indicated sales. They also tried using a paper tape rather than an adding mechanism to record sales. This machine, called "Ritty's Incorruptible Cashier," was the first the

Ritty brothers actually sold.

The Rittys found few takers for their machines, and sold their patent rights in 1881. The new manufacturers added a cash drawer to the machine, but were no more successful. In 1884, John H. Patterson, who had been one of the Rittys' first customers, bought up the business and named it The National Cash Register Company. Patterson had a gift for salesmanship, and a determination to create cash registers for businesses of all sizes. He also took a paternal interest in the welfare of his workers, introducing lunchrooms, required exercises, and lectures on nutrition. National Cash Register soon was a thriving business. In 1904, the copy of Ritty's Model Number 1 shown in Figure 29 was exhibited at the Louisiana Exposition in New Orleans as the starting point of a new industry.

References: Bernstein (1989), Marcosson (1945).

Figure 29. J. J. Ritty's Model I cash register. This is a copy of Ritty's original prototype. It was exhibited by NCR in 1904. The instrument has a wooden case and a metal face and mechanism. It measures $21^{3}/_{4} \times 14^{1}/_{2} \times 20^{1}/_{4}$ in. ($55.3 \times 37 \times 51.5$ cm). National Museum of American History Collections. Photo by Richard K. Hofmeister, Smithsonian.

Figure 30. An NCR cash register with a brass case, made in 1919. It measures $18^{3}/_{4} \times 15^{1}/_{2} \times 2^{5}/_{8}$ in. ($47.5 \times 39.5 \times 57.5$ cm). Note the numbers on top, the receipt printer on the left, and the cash drawer below. National Museum of American History Collections. Photo by Laurie Minor, Smithsonian.

Electromechanical Devices

A mechanical calculator handled numbers by an ingenious combination of cams, gears, levers, pins, and rods. The power required to operate it usually came from the user, who pulled a lever, turned a crank or pushed a key. For most machines of the nineteenth century this power was adequate, although it is interesting to note that Charles Babbage had proposed to power his never-completed Analytical Engine by steam. By the end of that century, the development of small, rugged electric motors made it possible to power some of the more complex calculators by electricity, in place of human muscles.

Electricity had an even greater potential as a carrier of information. Unlike mechanical elements, electrical wires can be arranged with great flexibility. Parts of an electrical device that perform related functions need not be physically close to one another. As inventors sought to build machines that did more than just the basic functions of arithmetic, they turned to electricity as a way to manage the complexity of their designs.

Using electricity for counting or figuring requires that the numbers or other information—represented in calculating machines by teeth in a gear or pins in a pinwheel— be coded as a sequence or pattern of electric currents. It also requires a way to transfer that information from one part of the machine to another—in mechanical calculators done by trains of gears or levers. The Morse telegraph of the 1830s, though not a calculating machine, showed the way this might be done. Samuel Morse developed for his system a code that represented the alphabet as a pattern of long or short pulses of current. The Morse code was not adapted for numerical processing, but subsequent inventors developed similar coding schemes to represent digits.

Morse and his associates also developed a device called a *relay*, which transferred electrical pulses from one circuit to another, while preserving the information coded in them. A drawing of an early relay from a Morse telegraph system is shown in Figure 31. The action of a relay is similar to the baton passes from runner to runner in a relay race: the individual runners, like the electrical currents of a telegraph system, are present for only parts of the race.

Grace Murray Hopper used the term "bug" to refer to flaws in the programming of the ASSC Mark I. Operators of the Mark II computer found a moth in their machine and taped it into the logbook with the comment, "first actual case of bug being found."

The baton, like the coded signals, makes the journey from beginning to end.

In the simplest form of relay, a coil of wire around a piece of soft iron becomes magnetized whenever there is a current present. Its magnetic field acts on a hinged piece of iron, which switches an electrical connection from one to another circuit. When there is no current in the coil, and no magnetic field, a spring draws the contact to its original position (see Figure 32). The action is similar to an ordinary light switch, with an electrical current instead of a person doing the switching. In the jargon of electrical engineering, the current that activates the magnet is called the *pickup*, the current that is switched the *common*, and the two circuit paths *normally open* and *normally closed*. It is a simple matter to provide the relay with a number of circuits, all opened or closed by the same pickup current. One may also arrange a set of contacts in a semicircle and remove the return spring. With this type of relay, each successive pulse of current on the magnet steps the common current from one contact to the next, eventually returning to the original connection.

Figure 31. A telegraph relay in the Morse system, as shown in Prescott (1860). A device like this one is in the National Museum of American History Collections.

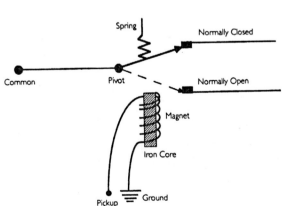

Figure 32. A simple relay. The presence of a current in the "pickup" wire polarizes the electromagnet, so that it attracts the pivoted switch. Current then flows from the "common" to the "normally open" wire in the lower circuit.

Telegraph engineers used relays to circumvent the inevitable current losses that would otherwise make a long-distance signal too weak to be read. The relay had an additional quality exploited by inventors of computing devices. Suitable combinations of simple relays could switch currents over a variety of other circuits, according to simple rules specified by a designer. For example, one could arrange a set of relays so that it allowed current to pass only when it received pulses from two channels simultaneously. Other sets of relays could act as gatekeepers, preventing a signal from passing unless a controlling signal was present, or opening up a circuit only when they received a specific number of pulses from another circuit, and so on.

One of the first to use this latter ability was Almon Strowger in 1890. He invented a system that automatically selected a telephone circuit based on the rotation of a dial connected to a bank of relays having ten positions each. For example, dialing the number "5" sent five pulses over a wire and advanced the Strowger relay five positions to make a connection to the fifth circuit. (Rotary dial telephones are still common throughout the world, although in the United States they have been largely replaced by push-button phones.) As telephone systems grew to a nationwide network, engineers devised sophisticated uses of relays not only to route a call by dialing numbers, but also to route calls automatically along one of several long-distance lines, to recognize and inform the caller if a line was busy, and to do other complex functions involving numbers and logical switching. All of this activity was a form of numerical processing. Representing numbers and information electrically has served the needs of census takers, cryptographers, and racetrack owners.

In the chapter that follows, we describe diverse objects that used electrical signals and electromechanical relays in computing. First, we consider the tabulating equipment developed for the U.S. Census of 1890, as well as tabulating equipment made by IBM in the 1930s. Next, we discuss a cipher machine known as the Enigma and a machine called the Bombe, developed to aid in deciphering Enigma messages. Both of these cryptographic devices used electrical signals to represent letters, and the Bombe had both relays and a small number of vacuum tubes. Then we discuss the totalisator or tote machine, a large electromechanical instrument used to calculate odds in pari-mutuel betting.

In the mid-twentieth century, relays were adopted by those doing complex computations. Three people suggested that relay devices could be programmed to carry out a sequence of calculations. They were the German air-

craft engineer Konrad Zuse, the physicist and applied
mathematician Howard Aiken of Harvard University, and
the mathematician George Stibitz of Bell Telephone Laboratories. All three of these inventors began work with their
own funds or aid from private industry. All found that
military agencies were much interested in computing
devices during World War II. All three built a series of
machines of differing size, components and capabilities.
We describe two of these electromechanical calculators
that survive, at least in part, in the Smithsonian collections. They are Aiken's ASCC Mark I and the Bell Telephone Laboratories Model V. With these instruments, the
electromechanical relay paved the way for the transforma-
tion of the mechanical calculating machine into the programmable computer.

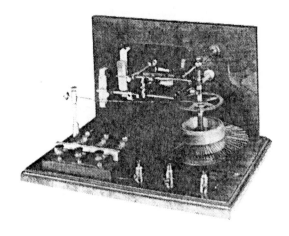

Figure 33. Almon
Strowger's 1891 patent
model of an electro-
mechanical switch. A
replica of this object is
at the National
Museum of American
History. The replica
measures $12 \times 8 \times 7\frac{3}{8}$
in. $(30.5 \times 20.4 \times 18.8$
cm). Photo courtesy of
AG Communications.

Herman Hollerith and His Tabulating System

The United States Constitution requires that every ten
years the national government take a count of the country's population. By 1880, there were so many people, and
the Census Office asked so many questions, that census
keepers could not keep up—detailed results from the 1880
census were not all available until 1888. Several inventors,
including a graduate of the School of Mines of Columbia
College named Herman Hollerith, sought machines that
would speed up the work.

When Hollerith (1860–1929) graduated from college
in 1879, he briefly went to work as an assistant at the Census Bureau. During the next decade, Hollerith spent a year
as an instructor at MIT, another year in St. Louis working
on improved brakes for railways, and some time in Washington, D.C., working as a patent examiner. Throughout

this time he worked on ways of mechanizing the census.

Hollerith became interested in machinery for census tabulation during his first stay at the Bureau. At this time, he discussed the problem with his associates, including John Shaw Billings (1838–1913), a distinguished medical administrator and Director of Vital Statistics for the 1880 census. The idea of using punched holes in cards or slips of paper to record census data may have arisen in a conversation with Billings. In 1884, Hollerith filed a patent on the "art of compiling statistics." He used equipment related to this patent to tabulate mortality statistics for the city of Baltimore in 1887. A revised patent application filed that year claimed the preparation of separate record cards as one of the improvements in compiling statistics. In the late 1880s, mortality records for New Jersey and New York were compiled on Hollerith equipment. He also exhibited his system at the 1889 world's fair in Paris. When it proved faster than those of two competitors, he was awarded the contract for the tabulation of the 1890 United States census.

Hollerith had not devised a single machine, but a system of machines that included a punch, a tabulator, and a sorting box (see Figure 34). Information received from census takers was punched onto blank cards. Holes on a card indicated such data as the sex, age, race, marital status, ancestry and occupation of one person. Punched cards were placed on a small press that was linked to the tabulating machine. Lowering the press lowered metal pins, which came down on all points on the card where there might be a hole. If the pin passed through a hole, it dropped into a small cup of mercury, closing an electrical circuit and advancing a hand on one of the counters of the tabulating machine by one. The Census Bureau wanted to tabulate data on various groups of the population. This required sorting out cards for the people of interest, and counting these again. The sorting box attached to the tabulating machine assisted in this task. It also was possible to wire relays at the back of the tabulator so that it counted an electrical signal only if several holes on a card were punched (for example, one could count only bachelor farmers of Norwegian extraction who lived in Minnesota).

Hollerith established his own company in Washington, D.C. After the 1890 census, he provided machines to various foreign governments for tabulating their census data. Hollerith also sought out large-scale businesses as customers, approaching railroads that needed to keep track of freight cars and life insurance companies that maintained files on individual policyholders.

References: Anonymous (1890), Austrian (1982), Martin (1891), Reid-Green (1989), Truesdell (1965), Willcox (1944).

Figure 34. The Hollerith tabulating system of 1890, as formerly exhibited. The tabulating machine in the center has its press in the front right center and counters across the back. The punch is on the left, the sorting box on the right. The tabulating machine alone measures, overall, $39\frac{1}{2} \times 32 \times 55$in. ($100.3 \times 81.5 \times 140$ cm). National Museum of American History Collections. Photo courtesy of Smithsonian.

Figure 35. The August 30, 1890 cover of *Scientific American*, showing the Hollerith tabulating system in use at the Bureau of the Census. Photo courtesy of Smithsonian.

In 1911, Hermann Hollerith's business, by then known as the Tabulating Machine Company, combined with two other companies to form the Computing-Tabulating-Recording Company (CTR). A few years later, Thomas J. Watson, who had been a highly successful sales executive at NCR, took over as president of CTR. In 1924, the company changed its name to International Business Machines Company (IBM).

Hollerith was not the only inventor of tabulating machines. During the early years of the twentieth century, a Russian emigré named James Powers designed new tabulating equipment for the U.S. Census Bureau. His machines counted and sorted data from punched cards, just as IBM equipment did. Powers machines represented numbers entirely by moving parts, not electrical currents. In other words, they were mechanical, not electromechanical (Powers equipment did have electric motors to drive its motion). In 1911, Powers left the Census to form the Powers Accounting Machine Company. In the 1920s, this firm joined with several other manufacturers to form Remington Rand, an ancestor of the present company Unisys. IBM and Remington Rand soon were fierce rivals, competing in the speed of their machines, the convenience of their design, and the readiness with which results were printed. IBM retained its confidence in relays, while Remington Rand insisted that its purely mechanical equipment verified and read cards, performed arithmetic, and printed results more accurately. In the 1950s, both companies would introduce tabulating equipment that operated electronically.

Encouraged first by Hollerith and later by Thomas J. Watson and the IBM sales force, a wide range of users adopted tabulating equipment. Railroads tracking freight, universities keeping records on students, insurance companies following policyholders, and astronomers forecasting the motion of the moon all resorted to punched cards. In the 1930s, economic depression led to new social programs, and with them new uses for tabulating machines. In 1935, the U.S. Congress passed the Social Security Act, legislation to aid retired wage earners. The new law required the government to keep records of the names, addresses and employment history of millions of Americans. In the first two months of 1937 alone, Social Security accounts were established for some 26,000,000 people. IBM produced and rented the machines that processed this information and punched the checks that served as Social Security payments.

Figure 36 shows two machines from the 1930s. The

first, a duplicating punch, was used to enter data on cards and to reproduce these cards as needed. The second is a horizontal sorter, introduced by IBM in 1925 and used to group together cards with common entries. The system also included a tabulating machine, which could produce a ledger sheet for individuals covered by Social Security. As mentioned, the Social Security checks themselves were printed on punched cards. Maintaining the files required over 200 card punches, some 79 sorters, and a smaller number of tabulating machines. During the same period, machines made under IBM and Remington Rand patents continued to sell abroad. For example, the German National Socialist government under Hitler made extensive use of punched card equipment in its registration of the population, both in Germany and in occupied countries. Special punched cards were prepared that described the physical characteristics of citizens and noted those who were Jews and gypsies. Those not fitting desired standards could then be singled out and sent to concentration camps.

Like Hollerith's machine, IBM tabulators of the 1930s read cards electrically and could count the number of cards with any desired combination of records. They also could add and subtract numbers, and print the results.

Figure 36. IBM tabulating equipment, a model 032 electrical duplicating punch and a model 080 horizontal sorter. The punch (shown on the right with a mannequin) measures 38 × 23¼ × 34½ in. (96.5 × 59 × 88 cm). The sorter on the left measures 57½ × 13⅞ × 45¼ in. (146 × 34 × 115 cm). Both are made primarily of iron and steel. On loan to the National Museum of American History. Photo by Rick Vargas, Smithsonian.

The Hollerith tabulator of 1890 represented numbers on clocklike dials. Later, Hollerith represented numbers on sets of adding wheels. By the 1930s, IBM tabulators contained compact electromechanical counters to record digits. Several of these counters were grouped together to represent a number. Like Hollerith's machine, the later tabulators used circuits containing relays to interpret the meaning of a combination of holes on a card being read. In Hollerith's time, setting the tabulator to count cards with a given combination of holes required soldering together an appropriate set of relays. This was time consuming and inconvenient. On the later machines, many tabulator circuits could be altered simply by changing cables that plugged into a board attached to the front. Changing circuits by moving cables in these so-called plugboards was much quicker and easier than resoldering wires.

Punched-card equipment was gradually displaced by electronic computers beginning in the late 1950s. Punched cards remained the medium for entering data into computers up through the 1970s. Moreover, the companies established to sell this equipment, and the markets their salesmen developed, played an important role in the formation of the computer industry.

References: Aly and Roth (1984), Aspray (1990), Austrian (1982), Comrie (1933), Connolly (ca 1967), Norberg (1990).

Ciphering and Deciphering—
The Enigma and the Bombe

During the 1920s and 1930s, as some developed machines to process data and to calculate, others invented devices to transform a message, letter by letter, into secret form. Such a message is called a cipher. One of the most important cipher machines, patented in the Netherlands in 1919, and developed by the German armed forces, was the Enigma. Figure 37 shows the form of the Enigma used by the German Navy. Typing a letter on the keyboard of this machine produced an electrical signal, which passed through a complex series of circuits and illuminated one of the letters in the alphabet behind the keyboard. The enciphered message was then transmitted by radio. Enigma circuits could be altered by changing the selection and placement of the disc-shaped rotors at the back of the machine, by altering the wiring of the plugboard at the front, or by adjusting the Uhr, an instrument attached to

Figure 37. A four-rotor German Navy Enigma cipher machine. It measures, with both front flap and lid open, 11¼ × 20 × 18 in. (28.5 × 51 × 46 cm). On loan to National Museum of American History. Photo by Rolfe Baggett, Smithsonian.

Figure 38. The American version of the Bombe. It measures approximately 10 × 2 × 7 ft. (approximately 3 × .6 × 2.5 m). An example is on loan to National Museum of American History. Photo courtesy of National Security Agency.

the plugboard. The setting of the machines was changed frequently, to make deciphering difficult for those without instructions on how to set them up (these instructions were known as the key).

By the 1930s, the government of Poland was worried about Germany's military plans. Their cryptologists followed changes in German ciphers carefully, figured out how the German Enigma worked, and built their own form of it. They discovered methods for deciphering Enigma messages by hand and, when the German machines became more complex, developed a machine to simulate several different Enigmas at one time. This electromechanical instrument, dubbed the Bomba, was completed by 1938. It emulated six German Enigmas simultaneously, and allowed the Poles to try out over 17,000 possible Enigma settings in two hours. Once the settings being used on a day were known, all the intercepted messages sent with that setting could be deciphered.

The Germans soon redesigned the Enigma, making the Polish Bombas inadequate. Moreover, in September 1939, Germany invaded Poland. Polish cryptographers fled to France and then Spain and passed on their knowledge of the Enigma, and their plans for the Bomba, to the French and the English. Cryptographers in England and the U.S. combined information from the Poles with their own techniques to build faster and more sophisticated forms of the Bomba or, as they called it, the Bombe. In Britain, the devices were built by the British Tabulating Machine Company, a firm that manufactured and sold punched-card equipment under IBM patents. In the U.S., Bombes were assembled by U.S. Navy personnel at NCR's factory in Dayton, Ohio. They then were shipped to the offices of the Signal Security Agency in Washington, DC. The first Bombes made in the U.S. were completed in the fall of 1943; over 120 were built. Figure 38 shows one of these machines. The American instruments were used especially for deciphering Enigma messages sent by the German Navy. Using information gathered in this way, allied forces were able to locate and attack German submarines, and hence keep supply lines open.

The Bombe did not perform calculations. Its success did create a demand for computing equipment among cryptographers. The British designed and built an electronic instrument known as the Colossus to assist in their work. The first of these was completed in February 1944, and ten were finished there by the end of World War II. Intelligence agencies became an important, if hidden, market for electronic computers. At the same time, several people involved in the design of the Bombe and the Colossus, such as the English mathematician Alan Turing, made important contributions to electronic computing after the war.

The Bombe and the Colossus were built and used in conditions of highest secrecy. Those who made and operated the machines were told a minimum about what they were doing and ordered not to tell others about their work. The general public did not learn the story of the breaking of the Enigma ciphers until the 1970s. Fuller accounts of the design and use of the Bombe and Colossus undoubtedly will emerge as more records are made public.

References: Andrew (1986), Aspray (1990), Hodges (1983), Kahn (1967, 1991), Kozaczuk (1984), Kruh (1985), Lewin (1978), Putney (1987).

The Totalisator

Electromechanical relays found a place in office work through tabulating machines. They appeared at the racetrack on computing devices called totalisators or, more informally, tote machines. In the nineteenth century, the French introduced the practice of letting the total amount bet on each horse running in a race determine the payoff for those who finished in the money (previously, a bookmaker set odds with each customer separately, in advance of a race. Hence bettors backing the same horse often received different payoffs if it won). This new system, called pari-mutuel betting, gradually spread throughout Europe and to New Zealand, Australia and the U.S.

People placing bets want to know what the payoff will be if their horse does well. For pari-mutuel betting, this requires finding the total sum bet on each horse in a race, computing the corresponding odds, and displaying these for all to see. By 1880, a few racetracks in New Zealand used hand-operated machines called totalisators to calculate the necessary sums. Just before World War I, the New Zealand railway engineer George Julius introduced a mechanical totalisator. It was powered by electricity, with numbers accumulated through the motion of a train of gears, and indicated on large rotating drums. There were no relays. This system not only calculated totals and indicated amounts bet, but included machines for issuing tickets to bettors. Julius's totalisator was adopted at various racetracks in New Zealand, Australia, Great Britain and South Africa.

In 1927, a Johns Hopkins University graduate and electrical engineer named Henry L. Straus won a bet at a Maryland racetrack, and was distressed to discover that his payoff was considerably less than the odds indicated just before the race. Perceiving a need for more rapid computations, Straus set out to build a totalisator that used electromechanical relays. By 1929, he and two engineers from the General Electric Company had designed a prototype and persuaded the British Race Course Betting Control Board to put it to use. In 1933, after the relay totalisator had come to be generally used in England, one of these machines was installed at Arlington Park, a racetrack near Chicago. Over the next decade, the ticket-issuing machines, totalisators and illuminated tote boards of Straus's American Totalisator Company (later Am Tote) became commonplace at American racetracks.

Figure 39 shows a small part of the room-sized American Totalisator model 7-C tote machine, introduced in 1940. Components of the machine were mounted on wheels, so they could be trucked from track to track in the course of a year. The totalisator, as its name suggests, added up the amount bet on each horse to win, place or show. Summing these totals, it also found the total pool bet on all horses in a race to win, place or show. From these totals, clerks using desktop calculating machines calculated the current odds. The numbers were updated every 90 seconds, and appeared on tote boards that overlooked the track. After a race, payoffs were computed on calculating machines using the final totals recorded on the totalisator. The reliability of electromechanical tote machines not only was essential to the racing industry, but foreshadowed the reliability of electromechanical devices built for quite different purposes, such as the ASCC Mark I and the Bell Telephone Laboratories Model V.

Straus also gave some thought to electronic computing devices. In the late 1940s, J.P. Eckert and J.W. Mauchly, designers of the ENIAC computer, started the Eckert Mauchly Computer Company (EMCC), which quickly faced financial difficulties. Warned of possible competition from electronic tote machines, Straus decided in 1948 that it would be prudent to invest in the firm. With backing from American Totalisator, EMCC completed the BINAC computer and continued development of the UNIVAC (see next chapter). However, in October 1949, Straus was killed in an airplane accident. Am Tote decided not to renew its loans to EMCC, and the latter company soon was acquired by Remington Rand. Totalisators remained electromechanical into the 1960s.

References: Anonymous (1931), Buck (1945), Liebowitz and Wolf (1973), Stern (1981).

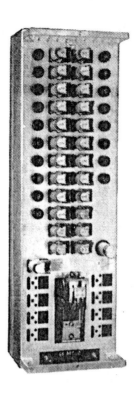

Figure 39. A bank of relays from a section of the American Totalisator Model 7-C. This section measures $8\frac{1}{4} \times 7\frac{1}{2} \times 26\frac{1}{2}$ in. (21 × 19 × 67.3 cm). It fits with nine other sections in a large metal cabinet, which is in turn only part of the machine. Photo by Pendergast and Wilkinson, Smithsonian.

Figure 40. A totalisator set up at Atlantic City, about 1959. Photo courtesy of Am Tote Division, General Instrument.

Figure 41. The ASCC Mark I, as installed at Harvard University. It was some 51 feet long and 8 feet high (15.5 × 2.4 m). It had some 750,000 parts, joined by over 500 miles of wire. Instructions and tabular information were entered on paper tape readers, with data supplied on punched cards or set on a bank of switches. Computations were carried out on 72 banks of rotary switches that were controlled and linked electrically. Results were printed out on electric typewriters. Portions of the machine are preserved at Harvard, at the National Museum of American History, and in the collections of IBM. Photo courtesy of Harvard University Cruft Photo Laboratory. Photographed by Paul Donaldson.

Electromechanical devices found a place in census offices, in business, among cryptographers, and at the racetrack. They also played a limited role in science, particularly at the Nautical Almanac Office in England and the Watson Astronomical Computing Bureau of Columbia University in New York. Born in New Jersey and raised in Indiana, the power engineer Howard H. Aiken (1900–1973) earned a Ph.D. in physics at Harvard University during the 1930s. Preparing his dissertation, Aiken performed numerous calculations on a desk calculator. He concluded that such work would be much easier if calculators could be programmed to perform a sequence of operations automatically. In other words, he envisioned a computer (some historians use the term "computer" to refer only to computing devices in which programs can be stored internally. In that sense, the ASCC Mark I was not a computer).

After he obtained his degree, Aiken remained at Harvard as a junior faculty member in physics. He approached the Monroe Calculating Machine Company about building the computing machine he envisioned, but they declined. In a 1937 proposal to IBM, he suggested that the technology of contemporary accounting machines—the decimal wheels and relays used in the punched-card equipment described above—might be extended for scientific use. Several changes were needed. Scientists worked with negative as well as positive numbers, often to much greater precision than the dollars and cents used in accounting. They also required a machine that handled functions such as logarithms, sines and cosines. Moreover, the machine needed a control mechanism that allowed one to carry out a series of calculations that involved different numerical values. In other words, it needed to be programmable.

Aiken, assisted by several of his Harvard colleagues, persuaded IBM to fund and build the new machine. IBM provided not only facilities at the company's development laboratory in Endicott, New York, but a group of experienced engineers. The machine these engineers built was called the Automatic Sequence Controlled Calculator. It later received the briefer name Mark I. The ASCC ran successfully in early 1943. The following year, it was moved to Cambridge and officially given to Harvard University. Figure 41 shows the ASCC Mark I installed at Harvard.

Figure 42. Howard Aiken examining a Mark I paper tape control reader, 1944. Photo from the Harvard University News Office. From the Science Service Collection, National Museum of American History.

During World War II, Aiken and his associates at Harvard joined the ranks of the U.S. Navy, and the Mark I was used for ballistics calculations. Several people who worked on the Mark I went on to distinguished careers as computer scientists. For example, the mathematician Grace Murray Hopper developed early programs for the Mark I, and prepared the section of the manual for the machine that described the electrical circuits. She went on to a distinguished career in private industry and government.

After the war, the Harvard Computation Laboratory published several volumes of tables of Bessel functions that were computed using the Mark I. The machine remained in use through the 1950s.

References: Aiken (1937), Ceruzzi (1983), Cohen (1992), Croarken (1990), Williams (1985).

Bell Labs Model V

At the same time that Howard Aiken worked on the Mark I, engineers at Bell Laboratories in New York City pursued a parallel course. Between 1937 and 1946 they built a series of digital calculators that used telephone relays for switching elements, and could execute a sequence of arithmetic operations that was coded into punched tape.

The inspiration for these calculators came from George Stibitz, a research mathematician at Bell Labs who had been working on improving the clarity and range of long-distance voice signals. That work involved calculations

Stibitz was first to use the word "digital" to describe computers. During World War II, on a panel advising the U.S. military on "analogue" and "pulse" computing devices, he suggested that the term "digital" was more descriptive than "pulse" for machines that counted in discrete units.

with so-called complex numbers—numbers that had two parts, one representing the strength of a signal, the other its phase relationship to time. Any amplification, transmission, or filtering of a voice signal had to take both into account. Mechanical desk calculators, to which Stibitz had access, could assist in these calculations but required lots of human time and effort. Stibitz suggested building a special-purpose calculator, using relays, to do these calculations automatically; working with Bell Labs engineer Sam Williams, he completed such a machine (later known as the Bell Labs Model I) in 1939.

With the onset of World War II, Bell Labs turned to a variety of war-related work, especially calculations related to the aiming and firing of antiaircraft guns. Stibitz proposed a new series of relay calculators that could be programmed by paper tape to do more than one type of computation.

The most ambitious of this series was the Model V, two of which were built in 1946 and 1947. This machine, consisting of 27 standard telephone relay racks plus assorted other equipment, represented perhaps the limit of what was possible with relay technology. By the time it was finished, most computer designers had come to prefer vacuum tubes, with switching speeds hundreds of times higher than relays. The Model V contained over 9,000 relays, had a memory capacity of 30 seven-digit decimal numbers, and took about a second to multiply two numbers together. Numbers were represented in floating point, a feature lacking in electronic computers for many years afterward, but one that was relatively easy to implement with multicontact relays.

Relays are reliable devices. They do tend to fail intermittently, often because of dust in the contacts. After a few cycles, the dust usually falls out, and the machine will run correctly again. Such malfunctions are very hard to detect; by the time someone looks for the faulty relay everything is working fine again. For a telephone system this is annoying but tolerable. For a calculator, however, one failure of this kind can ruin hours of work. The Model V had an elaborate system of built-in checking that would detect an error as soon as it occurred and automatically stop the machine. One could even program the Model V to switch over to another problem, mounted on another part of the machine, if it detected an error. Thus the machine remained busy in spite of a minor malfunction. Both these techniques resurfaced years later in the designs of advanced solid-state electronic machines.

Reference: Ceruzzi (1983).

Figure 43. The control panel of the Bell Telephone Laboratories Model V. This is only a small part of the device. The metal framework measures 30 × 8½ × 88½ in. (76 × 22 × 224 cm). National Museum of American History Collections. This BTL Model V was used by the U.S. Army for ballistics work at Aberdeen, Maryland, and then Fort Bliss, Texas. It later was transferred to New Mexico State University at Las Cruces. Portions of the machine came to the Smithsonian in the late 1960s. Photo by Diane L. Nordeck, Smithsonian.

Electronic Computers

When the first large-scale relay calculators appeared in the early 1940s, the world was engulfed in World War II. This war saw the development of weapons of enormous destructive power, a development intimately tied to the work of scientists and engineers. Warfare brought a sudden increase in the need for rapid, complex calculations in ballistics, aerodynamics, aircraft design, and the design of advanced weapons, including the atomic bomb. In the 1930s, inventors of relay calculators had to convince their peers that enough problems existed to justify the cost of these "giant brains." Lots of human brains needed work, and a few of them even found it doing arithmetic by hand. The Mathematical Tables Project, a Works Project Administration program in New York City, hired unemployed workers to do calculations and unemployed mathematicians to figure out how this could be done most effectively. Once the U.S. entered World War II, however, both relay computing projects like the building of the Mark I and human computers like those of the MTP were enlisted to tackle a mountain of urgent war-related work.

The electronic computer, like the atom bomb, was a product of World War II and the Cold War that followed. Early computers were large, expensive, one-of-a-kind devices, and only gradually became commercial products.

The war also brought new research on instruments that used vacuum tubes. Figure 44 illustrates the principle of the vacuum tube. It is an evacuated glass container in which electrons from a heated filament at the center (the cathode) are attracted to a positively charged plate (the anode). Current can flow only from the anode to the cathode. Vacuum tubes usually had a third electrode, known as the grid. Changing the voltage on the grid changed the flow of current in the tube. Negative grid voltages could stop the flow of electrons entirely, while positive ones might allow most or all of the electrons to reach the anode.

Engineers and physicists had explored the properties of tubes from the early twentieth century, and they were widely used in radio. War brought much more demanding applications of tubes, especially in radar, which transmitted pulses at frequencies much higher than those broadcast radios handled. Moreover, while a typical consumer radio might have five tubes, military radar and communications gear might have hundreds.

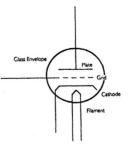

Figure 44. The standard symbol of a vacuum tube illustrates the principle of a triode tube. Electrons in an evacuated space flow from the heated cathode to the plate. The voltage on the grid controls this current.

Figure 45. Component from the EDVAC computer, interior view, with four vacuum tubes shown across the top in the photograph. Conceived in 1945 and completed in 1952, the EDVAC was built at the Moore School of Electrical Engineering of the University of Pennsylvania. These tubes are more complex than the triode schematic shown in Figure 44, having a cathode, an anode, and three grids. Because the tubes have a total of five electrodes, they are called pentodes. The component, which was only a small part of the computer, measures, overall, 9 × 2 ×10 in. (23 × 5 × 15.6 cm). National Museum of American History Collections. Photo courtesy of Smithsonian.

Two vacuum tubes may be joined in a circuit known as a flip-flop. Here components are linked so that when one tube conducts current, the other does not. Moreover, a new pulse of current switches the flow of electrons from one tube to the other. Current passing through one tube in a flip-flop circuit may be used to represent a "1," while current in the other tube represents a "0." Any number may be represented as a series of zeroes and ones. Thus flip-flop circuits could be, and were, used to count and accumulate numbers. Changing the flow of electrons in a vacuum tube flip-flop circuit takes much less time than opening or closing the contact of a relay. For this reason, counting circuits using vacuum tubes could switch much faster—up to a thousand times faster—than those with relays. Because electrons did the switching, machines using vacuum tubes and later transistors were called "elec-tronic."

By the 1930s tube counting circuits were already in use for at least one application where speed was necessary: counting cosmic rays entering the atmosphere. Relay counters simply could not keep up. Cosmic ray counters were relatively simple, and also did not need to be precise to the last digit, as a computer would have to be.

Electronic speeds came at a price. Tubes required much more power than relays. Designing reliable tube circuits was also more difficult. Early electronic computers used thousands of tubes, and each had to work reliably throughout the course of solving a problem. Although electronic computers were complex, their design was not that much more complicated than the design of an equivalent relay machine. For that extra effort one got a thousand-fold increase in computing speed. Even the reliability issue withered before that difference in speed: if one could get an electronic computer to operate reliably for even one hour (not an easy thing to do, it was true), one could do the same calculations that a relay machine like the Harvard Mark I, running day and night, would do in six *weeks*.

With the funds made available primarily from American and British military agencies, a number of engineers built electronic computers from the mid-1940s to the end of that decade. They had the money to work around the problem of vacuum tube reliability, operating tubes at considerably below capacity, replacing them systematically and, in some instances, encouraging manufacture of better components. Still, the vacuum tube's deficiences remained a check on the advance of computing system technology.

From the beginning of radio in the 1900s, engineers discovered that crystals of certain minerals had the property of passing electrical current in only one direction. Radio amateurs built inexpensive receivers that detected signals with a "cats whisker," that is to say a needle delicately placed on a crystal of lead ore. Physicists also explored the properties of such minerals. They found that some elements, especially germanium and silicon, sometimes conducted current and sometimes acted as insulators. They were "semiconductors."

Producing a solid-state device that could amplify or switch currents like a vacuum tube or relay proved difficult. Three physicists at Bell Laboratories finally succeeded in 1947. They called their new device a "transistor." It took a full decade of research and experimentation, accompanied by many false starts, before manufacturers learned how to make transistors that were as reliable, cheap, and uniform as vacuum tubes. The turning point came around 1960, when computer manufacturers began to produce and sell solid-state computers in large numbers, abandoning the vacuum tube altogether.

The high computing speeds of electronic devices also required new ways of programming—new techniques for supplying the machine with its sequence of instructions.

Figure 46. Two transistors from one of the first computers to use them, the Burroughs Atlas Model I Guidance Computer (1957). Transistors also were used in the IBM System/360. Photo courtesy of Smithsonian Institution.

Relay machines could be programmed by decks of punched cards or strips of perforated tape; the speed at which these delivered instructions was about the same as the speed the calculating circuits carried them out. Electronic computers required faster methods. The first electronic machines were programmed anew for each problem: wires connecting one part of the machine to another were plugged into plugboards, effectively rebuilding the machine to solve each problem. That worked fast enough, but it required long periods to set up every problem, during which the expensive computer sat idle.

It took a full decade of research and experimentation, accompanied by many false starts, before manufacturers learned how to make transistors that were as reliable, cheap, and uniform as vacuum tubes.

The solution to this programming problem was to store the instructions internally in the same high-speed memory that the computer used to store input data and the interim numbers produced while solving a problem. This idea, now known as the stored-program principle, marks a major breakthrough in the transition from calculators to modern computers. Internal program storage not only allows higher speeds, it also allows one to treat instructions as data, and perform operations on them. This opens up numerous possibilities. First, it allows a relatively simple program to handle a complex problem, one in which the sequence of instructions must change based on the results of a previous computation. Second, it allows a compact set of instructions to operate on large blocks or arrays of data. Such arrays are the norm in many scientific calculations, and are the rule in more prosaic "data processing" applications as well. Finally, the stored-program principle allows one to write programs in simple forms—using variations of ordinary English, for example—and let the computer operate on that program to transform it into the binary codes that are the only things a computer's

The stored-program principle marks a major breakthrough in the transition from calculators to modern computers.

electronic circuits can actually comprehend. It is no exaggeration to say that the present-day computer "revolution" would not have occurred had it not been for the development and implementation of this concept.

This chapter describes five pioneering electronic computers planned and built between 1942 and 1957. Three of these, the ENIAC, the IAS computer, and the Whirlwind, were one-of-a-kind machines, built at scholarly institutions, largely with U.S. government funds. The ENIAC was the first regularly operable general-purpose digital electronic computer. The IAS was among the first American machines to have stored programs. The Whirlwind not only carried out calculations extremely rapidly, but used an important new form of computer memory, a grid of magnetic cores. It also had one of the first interactive video computer displays.

Just as the name of Dorr E. Felt can be associated with the Comptometer and that of the Ritty brothers with the cash register, the names of engineers, mathematicians and physicists are tied to these machines. J.W. Mauchly and J. Presper Eckert led the team working on the ENIAC, John von Neumann, H.H. Goldstine, Julian Bigelow and James Pomerene directed the crafting of the IAS, and Jay Forrester and Robert R. Everett headed the group building the Whirlwind. However, these were much larger projects than their nineteenth or early twentieth century predecessors. They cost hundreds of thousands, or indeed millions, of dollars, and involved whole teams of people—designers, engineers, sponsors, programmers, operators, and users, to name only a few.

Two machines, the UNIVAC I and the IBM System/360, were commercial products. The U.S. government bought or rented some copies of both machines, but was not the only user. The UNIVAC was the first American computer produced commercially, while the IBM System/360 was perhaps the most successful computer of the 1960s. Historians and computer scientists have begun to sort out the complex commercial and technical debates behind the production of both of these machines. In general, however, the efforts of the individuals who designed and built them are even harder to untangle than those involved with the other computers discussed in this chapter.

The ENIAC

In the early twentieth century, electrical power networks were among the more complex engineering systems in use. In order to predict the performance of these systems, Vannevar Bush and associates at the Massachusetts Institute of Technology developed several analog computing devices. One of these, the differential analyzer, was sufficiently successful that copies were built at a few laboratories. At the outbreak of World War II, the U.S. Armed Forces contracted to use differential analyzers at MIT and at the Moore School of Electrical Engineering of the University of Pennsylvania. The machines were used to calculate firing tables for new artillery. Differential analyzers alone could not do the job. The government also hired people with the job title "computer" to calculate tables using mechanical desk calculators. This too proved inadequate. As the U.S. plunged deeper into war, the enormous need for firing tables produced a sense of crisis. John W. Mauchly (1907–1980) proposed that the University of Pennsylvania build an electronic, digital version of the analog differential analyzers that the Army was using. His proposal led to the ENIAC, completed in 1945, and regarded as the world's first successful general-purpose electronic computer.

Mauchly, born in Cincinnati in 1907, received a doctorate in physics from Johns Hopkins University in 1932. He was a gifted student, but finding a teaching position in those depression years was difficult. In 1934, Mauchly took a job at Ursinus College, in Collegeville, Pennsylvania, where he became, in his words, a "one-man physics department." He had a heavy teaching load, but also pursued research in weather forecasting, a topic that soon brought him up against a need for numerical calculation.

Mauchly explored various ways of mechanizing weather calculations. He accelerated his efforts after meeting Professor J.V. Atanasoff of Iowa State University at a scientific meeting, where he learned that the Iowa professor had similar interests and had begun preliminary work on a computing machine. In 1941, Mauchly visited Atanasoff briefly; at that time he also enrolled in a course at the Moore School to learn more about electronic circuits. There he met J. Presper Eckert, a young and talented electrical engineer. In August 1942, he and Eckert proposed a new computing project; the Army agreed to fund it the following June. The result was the ENIAC (Electronic Numerical Integrator and Computer), completed in 1945 and publicly unveiled in February 1946. Among historians, the influence of Atanasoff on Mauchly is a matter of dispute, and it seems likely that the dispute will continue. It does seem clear that by 1941 Mauchly was considering the feasibility of electronic computation and that his visit to Iowa would have encouraged such thinking. In any case, it was Mauchly whose drive and energy were essential to bringing the ENIAC, and with it electronic computers, into being.

The ENIAC initially did not store its programs in its internal memory, but it could carry out operations at electronic speeds. Operators set the machine to solve problems by plugging in cables and setting switches—in effect, rewiring the machine for each new problem to be solved. Punched-card equipment handled input and output of numbers, but could not be used to feed instructions into the ENIAC because it could not operate fast enough. The computer cost almost $500,000, and required six full-time technicians to keep it running. Each of the more than 17,000 vacuum tubes was checked weekly. In the first 11 months of 1949, when the machine was running regularly, about 2,000 tubes were replaced per month. About half of these were actually bad when they were replaced.

Some historians reserve the term "computer" for those programmable calculating devices that have stored programs. Under this definition, neither the Mark I nor the ENIAC as it initially operated was a computer. The first successful computing devices to have stored programming were built in England. A prototype device operating with stored programs was built at Manchester University in 1948. Both the Manchester Mark I computer and the EDSAC, a computer built at Cambridge University, were stored-program machines which first operated in 1949.

Figure 47. The ENIAC computer, installed at the Moore School of Electrical Engineering. The ENIAC was big. It weighed 30 tons and took up 1800 square feet of floor space. The entire machine contained over 17,000 vacuum tubes, 70,000 resistors, 10,000 capacitors and 6,000 manual switches. Photo courtesy of Science Service Collection.

Figure 48. Five of the sections of the ENIAC exhibited at the National Museum of American History. The initiating unit is on the left, the divider and square rooter next, then one of the computer's accumulators, and finally two high-speed multiplier panels. Several other parts of the machine also are on exhibit. National Museum of American History Collections. Photo by Laurie Minor, Smithsonian.

The ENIAC was completed in December 1945, after World War II had ended. Its first calculations were used in the design of atomic weapons and in ballistics work. It was used for many other applications, including the first numerical weather prediction by computer. In the fall of 1947, engineers disassembled the ENIAC and moved it from the University of Pennsylvania to the Army's Aberdeen Proving Ground in Aberdeen, Maryland. The installation at the Moore School is shown in Figure 47. Portions of the ENIAC were transferred to the Smithsonian in the early 1960s.

References: Anonymous (1953), Stern (1981), Williams (1985).

As the ENIAC neared completion, Eckert, Mauchly and others at the Moore School of Engineering talked about what they should do next. They consulted with John von Neumann (1903–1957), a Hungarian-born mathematician at the Institute for Advanced Study in Princeton, New Jersey. During the war, von Neumann played an important role in carrying out calculations used in the design of the first atomic bombs, and he was intensely interested in improving computing devices.

In June 1945, von Neumann prepared a synthesis of ideas being circulated at the Moore School. This was entitled "First Draft of a Report on the EDVAC," and it gave the first detailed description of a stored-program digital computer—a digital computer whose instructions were stored within the memory of the machine itself, and not just on an external device like a paper tape or plugged cables as with the ENIAC. With this scheme the Moore School group hoped the new machine, called the EDVAC, would be just as powerful as the ENIAC, yet smaller and easier to program.

The EDVAC (Electronic Discrete VAriable Computer), named in von Neumann's report, was to be built at the Moore School of Electrical Engineering. Von Neumann's report was the center of discussion at a conference held there in the summer of 1946, and several other stored-program computers were soon under construction. One of the most influential of these, the Institute for Advanced Study computer (IAS), was built in Princeton under von Neumann's direction. Funds for this machine came from the IAS, the U.S. Atomic Energy Commission, and several military agencies of the U.S. government; it cost several hundred thousand dollars. Designers of the IAS were required to make their plans available to several other government-funded projects so that they could build their own machines. As a result, several machines resembling the IAS were built, with names such as JOHNNIAC, MANIAC, AVIDAC, ORACLE, ORDVAC, and ILLIAC. These were not exact duplicates of one another, but followed the same general plan. Some early computers built abroad, such as the Australian SILLIAC, the Swedish BESK, and the Israeli WEIZAC, were patterned on the Princeton machine. The IAS also influenced the design of the IBM 701, the first electronic computer marketed by International Business Machines.

Begun in 1946, the IAS was ready for use in 1952. Arithmetic operations were carried out in parallel, speeding operations. The memory was a set of 40 phosphorescent cathode ray tubes, designed along lines suggested by

Figure 49. John von Neumann and the IAS computer. The IAS was considerably smaller than the ENIAC. It took up 100 square feet of floor space and had only 2300 vacuum tubes. The cylinders running along the base of the instrument are part of the cathode ray tube memory. Photo courtesy of Institute for Advanced Study Archives.

Figure 50. IAS computer, as formerly exhibited. The main section measures approximately 6 × 2⅓ × 10 ft. (approximately 1.8 × .75 × 3 m). National Museum of American History Collections. Photo courtesy of Smithsonian.

the British engineer F.C. Williams. A row of these cylindrical tubes appears along the base of the IAS, as one can see in Figure 49. After various trials, punched cards were used in both input and output.

Von Neumann wanted to discover new applications for computers, not simply do routine calculations. Users of the machine worked on problems of hydrodynamics, including some relating to the design of the hydrogen bomb. They also studied aspects of meteorology, number theory, astrophysics, and evolutionary biology. In 1956, the IAS computer was scheduled to move from the Institute for Advanced Study to the Princeton University campus. However, Princeton University decided that a commercially built computer would be more reliable and cost effective, and donated the machine to the Smithsonian Institution.

References: Anonymous (1953), Aspray (1991), Bigelow (1980), Goldstine (1972), Williams (1985).

A very influential early computer was the Whirlwind, designed and built between 1945 and 1953 at the Massachusetts Institute of Technology in Cambridge, Massachusetts. The computer was built as part of a project of the same name that explored new ways of controlling, analyzing, and simulating complex physical phenomena. Sponsored by the U.S. military, Project Whirlwind began in the closing months of World War II as an attempt to simulate an aircraft's performance while the airplane itself was still being designed. That would allow engineers to get a sense of how the plane would behave once built. The Navy also hoped to have a computing device that would simulate a variety of airplanes, old and new, for use in pilot training.

Meeting these specifications required a computing device that responded as fast as the physical system—in this case, an airplane—it simulated. Engineers described such a machine as capable of "real-time" operation. In 1945, only analog devices were capable of such speeds (real-time analog controllers are not all that rare: the camshaft and distributor of an ordinary automobile use rotating cams to control the flow of fuel and electricity in an engine in real time). However, by 1946 the director of Project Whirlwind, Jay W. Forrester, decided that a digital computer could be designed to work fast enough for real-time applications. The Whirlwind would be a stored-program, electronic digital computer.

Forrester's decision drove up the cost and complexity of the project, and, when the end of the war lessened the urgency of its goals, the Navy wanted to withdraw funding for the program. Then, in the summer of 1949, the Soviet Union successfully tested an atomic bomb. The newly formed U.S. Air Force took an interest in computers like Whirlwind as the nerve center of an early warning system that could detect Soviet bombers flying over the North Pole to the U.S. and direct Air Force planes to intercept them. The calculations required of such a system were daunting, and the computers had to operate in real time. Whirlwind seemed to have those abilities and, with Air Force funding, the project continued. The computer, occupying a floor of the Barta building on the MIT campus, began solving test problems in 1951, and by 1953 it was doing useful and important work.

In a series of tests conducted by the Air Force over Cape Cod in 1952, Whirlwind demonstrated its ability to control an aircraft warning and control system. Its success led to the massive SAGE system, a network of very large computers housed in windowless concrete bunkers across the United States and Canada and linked to radar stations,

Figure 51. A part of the Whirlwind computer, as installed in the Barta building at MIT. Jay Forrester is on the extreme left, facing the camera. The Whirlwind took up 3300 square feet of floor space and had 6800 vacuum tubes and 22,000 crystal rectifiers. The computer processed words of 16-bit length. This was much shorter than usual on computers of the time, and helped to speed operations. The machine could perform 42,000 additions or up to 25,000 multiplications per second. Portions of the computer, including several of its memory devices, are in the National Museum of American History Collections. Photo courtesy of MITRE Corporation Archives.

ships at sea, antiaircraft missile sites, and command centers in Washington. SAGE used computers based on the Whirlwind design, manufactured by IBM. The network operated from 1963 into the 1980s.

In its initial design, Whirlwind stored data in a bank of large vacuum tubes, in which individual bits were stored as tiny electrical charges. These tubes, similar to the ones used in the IAS computer, were unreliable. While some MIT engineers struggled to improve them, Forrester developed a way to store information on tiny, doughnut-shaped cores of magnetic material. The direction of magnetization of the core represented the binary number one or zero. Wires threaded through the hole in each core allowed one to read the number stored there, as well as to write a new number in its place. After much developmental work, useful core memory units were installed on Whirlwind in 1953. Core memory increased the speed and reliability of the machine dramatically. Core memory became standard in computers until the 1970s.

The development of high-speed circuits and core memory were only two contributions of the Whirlwind project . MIT graduate students and faculty members developed innovative programming techniques using the machine, including one of the first high-level programming languages, as well as systems for controlling industrial processes and machine tools, and for interactive graphics. Many of the founders of the "Route 128" electronics firms that grew up in Boston's northwestern suburbs were alumni of Project Whirlwind. Perhaps they were its greatest legacy.

The Whirlwind operated at MIT until 1959, and then ran for several years at a private firm in Massachusetts. Portions of it were received by the Smithsonian in 1966 and 1976.

References: Anonymous (1953), Everett (1980), Redmond and Smith (1980), Williams (1985).

The electronic computers discussed thus far—the ENIAC,
the IAS and the Whirlwind—were all one-of-a-kind
devices. Even the copies of the IAS were not exact duplicates. All of these machines were built to solve scientific or
military problems. They were not designed to assist with
data processing by business or government bureaucracies,
as earlier calculating and tabulating machines had been.
Moreover, early computers were funded by government
contracts, supplemented by individual initiative. They
were not commercial products. This changed with the
UNIVAC.

Soon after the formal dedication of the ENIAC in 1946,
J.P. Eckert and J.W. Mauchly left the Moore School of
Engineering to start their own business. Early orders from
U.S. government agencies and other potential customers
were not enough to keep the young Eckert-Mauchly Computer Corporation alive, and Remington Rand agreed to
purchase the firm in 1950. Work on the UNIVAC (UNI-
Versal Automatic Computer) went forward, and the first
of these machines, shown in Figure 52, was delivered to
the Bureau of the Census in early 1951. By 1957, some 46
copies of the machine had been installed at locations ranging from the David Taylor Model Basin of the U.S. Navy
Bureau of Ships, to Pacific Mutual Life Insurance Company, to the offices of the Commonwealth of Pennsylvania. Remington Rand was by no means the only company
building computers for commercial use. For example, the
English firm of Ferranti installed its first computer at
Manchester University slightly before Eckert-Mauchly
installed the first UNIVAC. IBM would not be far behind.
Nonetheless, the UNIVAC is an apt symbol of the beginning of the American computer industry.

The UNIVAC, like the ENIAC, had vacuum tube circuit elements. There also were some 18,000 crystal diodes.
Electrical signals were stored in the machine by generating
sound waves that passed through a tank of mercury. These
sound waves generated new electrical signals at a crystal at
the end of the tank. The signals were then amplified and
reshaped. Such acoustic delay-line memories, as they were
called, were used on several computers of the period.
There also was an external magnetic tape memory, as well
as magnetic tapes used in input and output. Users of UNI-
VAC played an important role in the development of programming languages.

References: Anonymous (1953), Lavington (1980), Lukoff (1979),
Stern (1981), Walker (1981), Williams (1985).

Figure 52. The first UNIVAC I computer, just after it was turned over to the Bureau of the Census in 1951. Parts of this machine are in the National Museum of American History Collections. The National Museum of American History also holds components of a UNIVAC I used in offices of the Commonwealth of Pennsylvania and parts of another machine, used by the Life and Casualty Insurance Company of Tennessee. UNIVAC installations varied in size, but filled a room approximately 25 × 50 ft. (approximately 7.6 ×15.2 m). Photo courtesy of Unisys Corporation.

Figure 53. Grace Murray Hopper and colleagues, getting the programming language COBOL to run on a UNIVAC computer. About 1960. Photo gift of Grace Murray Hopper.

International Business Machines, the manufacturer of tabulating machines that had its roots in Herman Hollerith's
Tabulating Machine Company, considered building electronic accounting machines before World War II. During
the 1950s, the company built a wide range of electronic
digital computers. These included machines for engineering applications like the IBM 701 (1952), business
machines like the IBM 650 (1954), and very large computers such as the AN/FSQ7 (1958), which was built for the
SAGE defense system. Between 1958 and 1960, IBM introduced computers in which vacuum tubes were replaced by
smaller, lighter, more reliable transistors. These were
intended for business (e.g., the IBM 1401), for scientific
and engineering applications (e.g., the IBM 7090), and for
large-scale computations (the STRETCH). Several
machines were very successful. The IBM 650 was the first
electronic computer installed in over 1000 locations, while
more than 12,000 copies of the IBM 1401 were produced.
Even the larger and more expensive IBM 7090 numbered
over 500 machines.

Different IBM computers had different central processors and required different spare parts. They ran different
programs, and had to be connected differently to peripheral devices such as card readers and printers. As the number and variety of computers increased, keeping all these
machines going became a complex task.

In early 1962, IBM decided to unify its product line.
The computers in the System/360 family, whether for
business or engineering, had compatible processors that
ran the same programs. Connections between computers
and peripherals were standardized. This not only made
things easier for IBM, it also created a market for other
manufacturers of devices that attached to IBM computers.

The memory capacity of each model of the 360
increased sufficiently so that it could not only operate the
new programs, but also run any programs written for a
lower model. IBM exploited a novel technique that
allowed the processors to be compatible across the line: it
designed for each model of the 360 a separate section of
high-speed, read-only memory known as the control
store. This store contained a sequence of so-called
microinstructions, or directions for indicating how the
processor was actually to carry out commands given by a
programmer. By tailoring these microinstructions, each
model's processor could be made to appear the same to a
programmer, despite differences in design and circuitry.

All the 360 computers used solid-state devices—transistors, resistors, diodes, and the like—mounted on small

squares of ceramic. These circuits were more compact than the individually wired circuits used in other computers of the day. By the time of the 360's introduction, computers using true "integrated circuits" (ICs) were already beginning to appear; a few years later IBM adopted the IC for its successor to the 360, which it called the IBM System/370. (The following chapter covers the development of the IC.)

By January of 1966, five models in the System/360 had been produced. Eight further versions would eventually be marketed. IBM had invested heavily in development of the new computers, and early delays in deliveries caused grave concern within the company about whether the risk would pay off. However, sales far exceeded predictions. By the end of 1970, almost 5000 IBM System/360s of Model 40 or larger had been placed. This was almost twice the 1964 estimate. Machines with remote terminals communicating to a central computer via telephone lines proved especially popular. Thus, for example, a terminal at a small college might be linked to a computer at a large university. IBM profits soared, and many of the principles developed in the design of the System/360 would be carried over into the company's later computers.

References: Evans (1986), Hurd (1981), Pugh, Johnson, and Palmer (1991), Williams (1985).

Figure 54. An IBM System/360/65 computer. A central processing unit, with attached control panel, from an IBM 360/50 is on loan to the National Museum of American History. This type of unit is in front of the seated figure in the photograph. It alone measures approximately 2½ × 4½ × 6 ft. (approximately .7 × 1.6 × 1.8 m). Photo courtesy of IBM Archives.

Flight Control
and Minicomputers

By the mid-1960s advances in electronics technology, coupled with a new set of demands largely driven by the cold war and the space race, led to a new class of digital computers very different from the "mainframe" installations represented by the IBM System/360.

What distinguished these machines was a combination of small size, low cost, and processing speeds as fast as those of mainframes. That combination suited them well for gathering and reducing data from a scientific experiment, or as a controller embedded into a larger system such as a telephone switching network or a power plant. These devices came to be called "minicomputers"; the name probably came from the Morris Mini Minor, a very successful British automobile also introduced around 1960. Whether that was the origin of the name or not, the success of both products was due to the same combination of factors: low cost, compact size, and performance equal to or better than the larger products they competed with.

The minicomputer's performance was a result of advances in packaging, transistor performance, memory technology, and basic design. Above all, the minicomputer's design took full advantage of recent innovations by electronic engineers in basic circuit design.

In the late 1950s, two engineers, Jack Kilby of Texas Instruments and Robert Noyce of Fairchild, independently invented a method of placing many individual devices onto a single sliver of material, resulting in what Fairchild called the Integrated Circuit. They and their colleagues also developed ways of manufacturing these "chips" by photolithography, which allowed them to reduce their size and to mass-produce them cheaply once the initial design was worked out. Integrated circuit production was now almost like printing a newspaper, although the process was much more delicate, and it was not easy to get a good yield. By the mid-1960s this process became competitive with older techniques of using discrete circuits. Integrated circuits became the key to the success of the minicomputer and set the stage for the personal computer phenomenon that would sweep the industry in the 1980s.

As the minicomputer was enjoying success in the commercial market, a related phenomenon was occurring in the field of aircraft and rocket guidance. Air and spacecraft use numerous devices that assist in their control, guidance, and navigation. Most of these employ electronics, although hydraulic and mechanical controls were at one time more common. These devices "compute," but they are not the general-purpose machines that one usually associates with the term "computer." Because of the size and power requirements for computers carried on an airplane or rocket, they do not look anything like those found in ground-based activities.

The aerospace community refers to the devices that use electronic circuits as "avionics," short for "aviation electronics." Avionic boxes usually contain computer chips, but whatever information processing they do is overshadowed by their input-output functions. These are performed by radar and radio equipment, specialized cockpit displays, precision gyroscopes, hydraulic systems, and so forth. Avionic computers are at the opposite end of the spectrum from general-purpose digital computers found on the ground, in which the input-output facilities are seldom more than a keyboard, video monitor, and printer. For most of its history, aeronautical computing was a matter of special-purpose analog devices. That began to change in the 1960s, as electronic digital computers reached a level of performance and reliability that surpassed their analog brethren. Especially with the invention of the integrated circuit, aerospace engineers at last found it possible to exploit the power of digital computers, while keeping weight and size down.

This chapter begins with the most famous of the early minicomputers, the PDP-8, then shifts to the aerospace field, where the Gemini, Minuteman, and Apollo guidance and navigation systems are discussed. It returns to the commercial arena with the VAX computer, the most successful minicomputer of all.

The best-known example of a "black box"— the flight-data recorder that tells investigators what may have caused an airplane crash— is probably the only avionics that is not literally black. It usually is painted bright orange to help locate it after a crash!

In 1957 Ken Olsen and Harlan Anderson founded a company called Digital Equipment Corporation (DEC) with the goal of manufacturing and selling high-speed digital circuits. By 1959 the company was well established, and it introduced its first computer, the PDP-1 (The letters stood for "Programmed Data Processor"). The PDP-1 incorporated some of the engineering advances that would later characterize minicomputers, especially in its internal design and attractive packaging. About 50 were produced; its price was $120,000. DEC soon designed and began selling other machines as well.

Depending on their intended use, the early DEC computers were designed with a variety of "word lengths" (the number of binary digits the computer's internal circuits handled at a time). The company's engineers, however, concentrated on designing a processor that used a much shorter word than common at the time. That would give them a machine that operated as fast as any other, but it would be much cheaper, since its short word length simplified internal circuits. For arithmetic calculations the short word was a handicap, but DEC engineers recognized that many applications required as many or more controls as arithmetic operations—and these did not require a long word length.

In 1962 DEC, working with MIT's Lincoln Laboratories, developed the LINC, a computer with a 12-bit word length that was intended for use as a laboratory controller and computer for a single researcher. In that sense it was a personal computer, although, at a cost of $43,000, few individuals could afford one. The machine was well regarded by those who used it, but Digital Equipment Corporation did not aggressively market it. A few dozen were sold. However, experience with it led Digital to introduce a line of machines shortly thereafter that would inaugurate the class of minicomputers.

In 1963 DEC introduced a less expensive 12-bit machine, the PDP-5, and then, in 1965, the much improved, smaller and still cheaper PDP-8. The first model of the PDP-8 sold for $18,000. New versions of this machine that incorporated improvements in electronics appeared over the next decade. These became steadily smaller and cheaper, triggering a rush of new applications in which the computer was embedded into another system and sold by a third party (called an Original Equipment Manufacturer, or OEM). Some machines were specifically designed for time sharing and for business applications. Ultimately over 50,000 PDP-8s were sold (excluding those embedded as single chips into other systems).

The term "minicomputer" was probably coined by John Leng, head of DEC's U.K. operations in the early 1960s. He sent "minicomputer reports" back to headquarters, inspired both by the miniskirt, then coming into vogue in London, and the Morris Mini-Minor, a small car introduced in 1959 and enjoying phenomenal sales at the time.

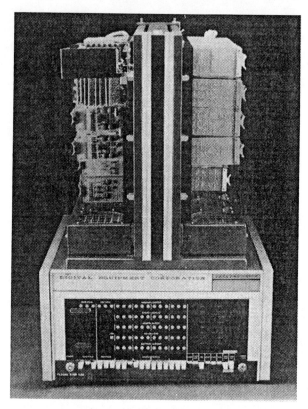

Figure 55. An early PDP-8, ca 1965, from the collections of and on exhibit at the National Museum of American History. The machine measures 20½ × 20½ × 32½ in. (52.1 × 52.1 × 82.5 cm). Plexiglas dust covers have been removed to reveal the circuit boards plugged into the vertical "backplane" that forms the spine of the computer. Note that early PDP-8s used discrete transistors. Later models used integrated circuits, and it was the development of the IC that helped drive the minicomputer market. Below the circuit boards are switches and lights that correspond to the binary digits contained in the registers of the computer's central processing unit. Photo by Laurie Minor, Smithsonian.

Among other early manufacturers of minicomputers were Computer Control Company (later a division of Honeywell), Interdata (later a division of Perkin-Elmer), and Varian Data Machines (later a division of Sperry Univac). The number of minicomputer manufacturers expanded rapidly in the late 1960s and early 1970s, as integrated circuits replaced both transistors and magnetic cores in the computer's processor and memory.

References: Bell, Mudge, and McNamara (1978), Bell and Newell (1971), Kenney (1978), Voelcker (1988).

Gemini Guidance Computer

Project Mercury was the United States' first manned space program. It had one basic goal: to get a man into space and return him safely to Earth. The Mercury capsule itself contained no on-board computer and flew an unpowered, ballistic trajectory once put into orbit. Except for returning to Earth, there was little the astronaut could do to alter his flight path. Project Gemini, first flown in 1965, inaugurated the use of digital computers as part of manned spacecraft. Gemini's mission was to test techniques of rendezvous in space with other craft—a tricky procedure but one that was crucial to a successful mission to the moon. Gemini's two-person crews thus were given the ability to alter their orbits.

Throughout the 1960s NASA sought to use ground-based computers to handle as much of the computing requirements of a manned mission as possible. Gemini's mission strained the limits of that policy. Because the mechanics of orbital rendezvous required constant calculations over fairly long periods of time, the Gemini capsule carried an on-board digital computer. Thus the Gemini missions inaugurated the use of digital computers as integral parts of manned spacecraft.

The Gemini computer had a 39-bit word length. A simple operation such as addition took 140 milliseconds, a multiplication took 420 milliseconds—almost half a second. It used discrete transistors, weighed about 60 pounds (27 kg), and was squeezed into a corner of the cramped Gemini capsule in a two-cubic-foot space to the left of the Commander's seat. Its memory was made of ferrite cores and held 4,000 words. Beginning with the Gemini-8 mission in March 1966, a magnetic tape unit was added for storage of additional programs. The computer was designed and built by IBM's Federal Systems Division at their Owego, New York, plant. A total of 20 were built between 1963 and 1965; half of these flew on manned missions.

Reference: Tomayko (1987).

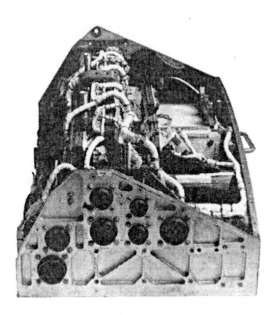

Figure 56. Gemini digital computer. The computer shown here is from the spacecraft flown by Wally Schirra and Tom Stafford during the Gemini-6 mission in December 1965. It is now on exhibit at the National Air and Space Museum. Dimensions are 18 × 15 × 13 in. (46 × 38 × 33 cm). Photo by David Dempster.

Because of their specialized nature, most aerospace computers have little influence on developments in the commercial world. But there have been several notable exceptions where military-sponsored projects have led to civilian spin-offs, especially in the area of circuit manufacturing and production. The most significant has been the Minuteman ballistic missile project sponsored by the U.S. Air Force.

Minuteman is an intercontinental ballistic missile designed to carry nuclear bombs to targets thousands of miles away from launch sites in the United States. A "ballistic" missile propels its warhead to a target on a free-fall trajectory, like a rock, after being boosted by its rocket engines. The term comes from a Roman engine that hurled rocks at enemy fortifications. For this concept to work, the rocket must be guided with great precision during the initial seconds of flight while the engines are still burning. Therefore the development of a guidance system is one of the more critical and difficult tasks facing the rocket designer.

The Minuteman uses an inertial guidance system. This technique measures the accelerations along all three axes of motion as the rocket ascends, referring those measurements to a reference plane kept fixed by a set of gyroscopes. An on-board computer integrates the measured acceleration twice with respect to the time of launch. (Integration is an operation of the calculus. In graphical terms, to integrate an equation is to measure the area under the curve traced by the graph of it). The first integration gives the rocket's velocity, the second its position relative to its starting point. The computer compares that position with the desired trajectory, and issues correcting signals to the rocket motors if necessary. Inertial guidance can provide the rocket's position in space without any reference to the outside world, a fact that makes it attractive to weapons designers. But to achieve any meaningful accuracy it requires gyroscopes and accelerometers of extreme precision, as well as a computer that can operate at high speeds.

As the U.S. policy toward the Soviet Union evolved, a new requirement emerged: to be able to change the missile's designated target up to the last moments before launch. Air Force crews, stationed underground next to the missile silos, would make these changes by sending new commands to the missile's guidance computer. For this "Minuteman II," the existing guidance computer was inadequate. In 1962, engineers decided to use the newly invented integrated circuit for the Minuteman II's com-

Figure 57. Minuteman III guidance ring. The National Air and Space Museum has on exhibit a Minuteman III, a slightly more advanced version of the Minuteman II. The photograph shows the guidance ring for a Minuteman III, also on display. The computer is the rectangular box on the right. The ring is positioned between the upper stage and the nose cone containing the warhead. The five-foot (1.5 meter) ring was built by the Autonetics division of North American Aviation (now Rockwell International). Photo by Mark Avino, Smithsonian.

Figure 58. A Minuteman II being launched from Vandenberg Air Force Base, California. U.S. Air Force photo.

puter to gain more processing capability. That project became the first significant order for production quantities of chips. From 1962 through 1965 Minuteman was the largest consumer of the industry's output of chips and accounted for 20% of the industry's sales in dollar value. Each Minuteman II computer used about 2,000 integrated circuits, and the Air Force contracted for hundreds of missiles.

The Air Force order established the integrated circuit as the best of many competing ways then being proposed to shrink electronic circuits. In economists' terms, the Minuteman II contract drove the chip down the "learning curve," as manufacturers learned the art of making them in quantity. The result was that the integrated circuit, which started out as a delicate and expensive device, eventually became cheap and rugged. The revolution brought on by this sudden availability of cheap computing power is still being felt throughout modern society.

With the end of the cold war there has been a reduction in the numbers of nuclear-tipped ballistic missiles deployed around the world. It should be noted, however, that Minuteman missiles are still deployed in silos across the western United States.

References: Ceruzzi (1989), Linvill and Hogan (1977).

On July 20, 1969, Neil Armstrong and Edwin Aldrin steppped out of a fragile craft called the Lunar Module or "Lem" and onto the Moon's dusty surface. Circling overhead in orbit around the Moon was fellow astronaut Michael Collins aboard the Command Module. The Command and Lunar Modules each carried a digital computer on board. The one on the Lunar Module was the first to operate in "real time" as an integral part of the controls of a flying machine. The Command Module's computer assisted with the complex job of navigating through space.

The Apollo astronauts needed a computer to help them carry out maneuvers when they were behind the Moon and out of contact with the Earth. Also, the final descent to the Moon's surface was too delicate to be handled by a human being unassisted, and the several-second delay in any round trip of radio signals across space was too long to permit active control of the landing from Earth. Finally, the Command Module's computer served as a backup to the ground systems for navigation from Earth to the Moon.

To meet the demands of a lunar mission, NASA turned to Charles Stark Draper (1901–1987) of the MIT Instrumentation Laboratory in Cambridge, Massachusetts, who had a strong prior record of developing guidance systems for ballistic weapons. He proposed a system that used two identical computers, called Apollo Guidance Computers, for the Command and Lunar Modules; the computer on each was separately programmed for its respective task. Each computer weighed about 70 pounds (32 kg), was housed in a rectangular aluminum case, and communi-

Figure 59. Apollo Guidance Computer. The photograph shows one of the computers, with the DSKY on the right, removed from a spacecraft. The National Air and Space Museum has several Apollo computers in its collection, including some installed in their original Apollo craft that have flown in space. Dimensions: 6 × 24 × 16 in. (15 × 61 × 41 cm). Photo by Mark Avino, Smithsonian.

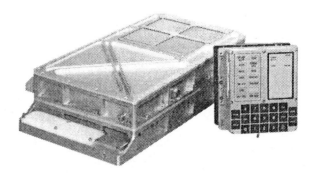

cated with the astronauts through a keyboard and display unit called a "DSKY." The Raytheon Corporation, of Sudbury, Massachusetts, eventually produced a total of 75 machines, using the Instrumentation Laboratory's design. The computer had a 16-bit word length, 36,000 words of fixed, read-only memory, and just 2,000 words of erasable memory. The computer's clock speed was 11.7 milliseconds. Programs were stored by a pattern of wires threaded through a bank of magnetic cores; a wire threaded through the hole in the core represented a binary "one," if threaded around the hole a "zero."

Designers at the Instrumentation Lab chose integrated circuits for the computer, barely three years after the IC's invention. A simple IC, containing three transistors and four resistors, was designed, and prototypes were supplied by Fairchild Semiconductor, the company where co-inventor Robert Noyce worked. Philco-Ford supplied the chips for the production models of the machine, at a cost of about $25.00 each—down from the $1000 each that Raytheon paid for the first few chips it bought for testing. Each Apollo computer used about 5000 chips. As with the Air Force's Minuteman project, NASA's contracts with Fairchild and Philco drove the cost of the chips down, thus spinning off the technology to the commercial and eventually the consumer market. By the time of the last Apollo flight in 1975, chip technology had advanced so rapidly that consumers could buy inexpensive computers that had as much capability as that carried on the Apollo capsule.

References: Ceruzzi (1989), Hall (1982), Tomayko (1987).

Figure 60. Location of Apollo Guidance Computer, display and keyboard (DSKY), and optical systems in a Command Module. Photo: Charles Stark Draper Laboratory, MIT

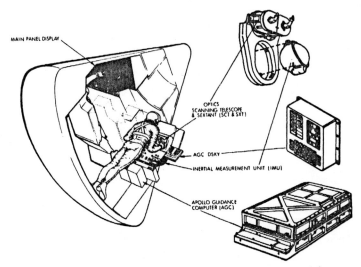

MAIN PANEL DISPLAY

OPTICS SCANNING TELESCOPE & SEXTANT (SCT & SXT)

AGC DSKY

INERTIAL MEASUREMENT UNIT (IMU)

APOLLO GUIDANCE COMPUTER (AGC)

M.I.T. CHARLES STARK DRAPER LABORATORY • Cambridge, Massachusetts •22930-1 • 9/70

Digital Equipment Corporation followed on the success of their PDP-8 with an equally successful 16-bit machine they called the PDP-11. By the mid-1970s it was clear that the short word length, a defining characteristic of the mini, was beginning to limit its use. The PDP-11's 16-bit word length meant that the central processor was unable to access more than about 65 thousand (2^{16}) words of memory at a time. The solution was to double the word length to 32 bits, while at the same time retaining the features of speed, low cost, and ease of use that had made the minicomputer so popular in the first place. Several companies introduced 32-bit minicomputers, which for a while were called "superminis" owing to their longer word length. Digital Equipment was not the first, but their 32-bit "VAX-11," introduced in 1976, became the most popular. The acronym stood for "Virtual Address Extension" of the PDP-11, reflecting the fact that the VAX was able to run most of the popular PDP-11's programs unchanged. That helped ease the transition to the new machine for many customers. As with earlier minicomputers, DEC continually brought out smaller and cheaper versions of the VAX in the following years, as well as models with improved performance at the high end. The VAX series eventually became one of the most successful designs in history.

References: Bell, Mudge, and McNamara (1978).

Figure 61. Digital Equipment Corporation MicroVAX II. The photograph shows a Digital Equipment Corporation "MicroVAX-II," a compact version of the VAX introduced in 1985 as a replacement for the original VAX line. Dimensions are 28 ×13 × 25 in. (71 × 33 × 64 cm). It is installed and can be viewed in the National Air and Space Museum's exhibit: "Beyond the Limits: Flight Enters the Computer Age." There it controls a variety of visitor-interactive displays. Photo by Carolyn Russo, Smithsonian.

Electronic Calculators

In 1983 *Time* magazine chose the computer for its "Machine of the Year" award, recognizing that a machine that had once been of interest only to accountants and scientists was now pervasive across all segments of society. The first hint of that cataclysm—that this machine was going to affect masses of people—came about a decade earlier, in the form of electronic calculators: machines which extended the traditional notion of the computer as a machine only for numerical work. What made their social impact so different was that these calculators were dramatically small and inexpensive. Within a few years beginning around 1972, what had previously been an exotic device suddenly became a commodity, used and relied upon by the full spectrum of society.

Beginning in the late 1960s, a few engineers toyed with the idea of building small computing devices that could be operated by a single individual. This became a more realistic and less expensive possibility as electronic circuitry became more compact. After integrated circuits entered the market in the late 1960s, the idea became even more compelling. By the mid-1970s it became possible to design a silicon chip on which was placed the entire central processing unit of a computer. Such a chip, called a microprocessor, needed additional circuitry to form a computer, but it gave engineers the freedom to design sophisticated yet inexpensive machines, without having to worry about the myriad details of processor design.

The pocket calculator soon appeared in a variety of configurations. Some, from companies like Hewlett-Packard and Texas Instruments, had calculating abilities that rivaled those of the largest computers of only a decade earlier. Others, especially those produced in Japan, were inexpensive machines that calculated only the four operations of ordinary arithmetic. Answers might be printed on a narrow paper tape, as with the Canon Pocketronic (1970), or be shown with light-emitting diodes, as on one model of the Busicom Handy (1971), or use a liquid crystal display, as with another model of the Handy. Along with digital watches, games, and other inexpensive consumer products, they soon flooded the market. Except

At first, only wealthy students could afford pocket calculators; others had to make do with slide rules. There was a risk involved. Early calculators were heavy users of batteries, and an unprepared student might suddenly find the display flickering and going blank during an exam.

Many executives prefer the appearance of analog watches. Hence manufacturers have made watches with an analog dial that flips up to reveal a calculator underneath. A few CEOs of personal computer companies defy corporate convention and sport digital watches.

Figure 62. Keyboard for the "Green Machine." Photo by Rolfe Baggett, Smithsonian.

Figure 63. HP9100A prototype. The photograph shows the prototype for the 9100A, based on the design of the "Green Machine." The HP9100A sold for under $5000, could be programmed using a keyboard or with wallet-sized cards, and was used primarily by scientists and engineers. The machine shown here is from the National Museum of American History Collections. Dimensions: 8⅝ × 15⅝ × 6½ in. (22 × 39.5 × 16.5 cm). Photo by Rolfe Baggett, Smithsonian.

for a few expensive models of scientific calculators, these machines were not programmable. But they did give the consumer a glimpse of the power of digital electronics.

This chapter begins with the "Green Machine" and its successor, the Hewlett-Packard 9100A—two prototypes of desk-sized electronic calculators. It then describes the HP-35: a pocket scientific calculator whose introduction in 1972 revealed the potential consumer market for digital electronics. Two inexpensive pocket calculators, made by Bowmar and Texas Instruments, represent the further penetration of digital electronics into everyday life. Finally, we describe a more recent pocket calculator, an HP-41C, that has been used by astronauts aboard the U.S. Space Shuttle.

Beginnings: The Green Machine

In 1964, Thomas E. Osborne, a founder of a company called Logic Design, used some of his leisure time to build a prototype electronic calculator. The "Green Machine," known for its color, had some 2264 diodes and 208 transistors, and could multiply more rapidly, over a larger range of numbers, than any desktop calculator then available. Osborne became a consultant to Hewlett-Packard, and his homebuilt device was refined and improved by that company into the HP9100A desktop electronic calculator, introduced to the public in 1968. Hewlett-Packard went on to build calculators with printed as well as electronically displayed output that were programmed using algebraic languages.

References: Gupta and Toong (1985), House (1988).

By the early 1970s, integrated circuits could be packed with enough components and manufactured with sufficient reliability to be marketed in handheld calculators. Early handheld calculators were sold by the Japanese firms of Busicom and Canon (Hayakawa Electric) as well as by U.S. makers such as Bowmar and Hewlett-Packard. At first, the prices were high. The Canon Pocketronic, Busicom, and Handy sold for about $400 in 1971; the Bowmar for $240. In 1972, Hewlett-Packard stunned the market when it introduced the HP-35 for $395. It was a remarkably sophisticated calculator that handled numbers in floating point (sometimes called "scientific notation") and stored and retrieved numbers automatically in a "stack" of four registers, just like some mainframe computers of the day. It not only could add, subtract, multiply and divide, but could be used to find trigonometric functions such as the sine and cosine, to find the reciprocal of a number, and to compute logarithms, exponents and powers. Scientists and engineers did not hesitate buying them—and in doing so relegated the familiar slide rule to the dustbin of history.

Reference: House (1988).

Figure 64. HP-35 pocket calculator (1972). Hewlett-Packard's first pocket calculator, the HP-35, was designed for scientists and engineers. Its name derives from its 35 keys. Dimensions: 3¼ × 5¾ × 1 in. (8.2 × 14.5 × 2.5 cm). William Hewlett, co-founder of the company, set the dimensions of the machine when he insisted that it fit in his shirt pocket. Fortunately for the HP-35's designers, Hewlett, a tall Coloradan, wore a good-sized shirt. From the National Museum of American History Collections. Photo by Brenda Gilmore, Smithsonian.

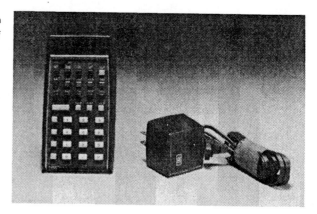

Figure 65. An early Bowmar calculator, from the National Museum of American History Collections. For a while the most popular and ubiquitous of the inexpensive pocket calculators was the Bowmar "Brain." It became the subject of numerous cartoons and jokes, and one was even featured in the hit Broadway play *Same Time Next Year*. In the movie version released in 1978, Alan Alda played the role of an accountant, who used the Bowmar to tally up his trysts with his mistress, played by Ellen Burstyn. The Bowmar performed simple arithmetic, displaying answers of 8 to 10 digits. The Bowmar shown here is from the collections of the National Museum of American History. Dimensions: 3 × 5¼ × 1½ in. (7.6 ×13.3 × 3.8 cm). Photo by Laurie Minor, Smithsonian.

Figure 66. A Texas Instruments SR-10 calculator (1972). Texas Instruments, which had manufactured the chips used in early Canon and Bowmar calculators, soon introduced its own "electronic slide rule," the SR-10 (1972). Texas Instruments was almost alone among American manufacturers in remaining in the business of making and selling cheap calculators and watches. Dimensions: 3 × 6⅛ × 1½ in. (7.6 ×15.5 × 3.8 cm). Photo by Brenda Gilmore, Smithsonian.

Inexpensive Pocket Calculators

Not long after their introduction, the prices of calculators dropped, at first slowly, then drastically to a point where the calculator cost less than its replacement batteries. Sales rose into the millions. Calculators became ubiquitous, appearing not only in laboratories and businesses but in ordinary homes and in combination with such personal items as key chains and watches. Elementary schools and even some colleges banned them from the classrooms, fearing an erosion of reckoning skills among children. These bans withered in the face of a market flooded by cheap machines, although there is evidence that the feared loss of skills has in fact happened. Severe competition drove early manufacturers, including Busicom and Bowmar, to bankruptcy. Typically, these machines handled the four functions of ordinary arithmetic, and perhaps also had a single memory register to store intermediate results.

Reference: Gupta and Toong (1985).

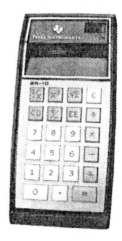

As unchecked competition drove many manufacturers out of business, Hewlett-Packard resisted the trend to lower prices, choosing instead to continue with high-priced calculators that had ever-more features and functions. Among their most successful was the HP-41C, introduced in 1979 at a base price of $300. It could be programmed to do a series of calculations, even choosing among several sequences of program steps depending on the results of a previous calculation. Programmable calculators like the 41C forever blurred the distinction between calculator and computer.

Reference: Jarett (1984).

Figure 67. An HP-41CV programmable calculator. The calculator shown here is a slightly more advanced model introduced in 1981. It had more memory than the original 41, and it also had a built-in timer. The liquid crystal display (LCD) could show letters of the alphabet as well as numbers—unusual in a calculator. The 41CV shown here was donated to the National Air and Space Museum by NASA. Before its retirement by the space agency, this calculator was flown on nine Space Shuttle missions between 1982 and 1985. A NASA technician purchased it at a Houston department store and made only minor physical modifications to it (such as putting pieces of Velcro on its case) before turning it over to the astronauts. It is now on display. Dimensions: 3¼ × 5¾ × 1 in. (8.2 × 14.5 × 2.5 cm). Photo by Mark Avino, Smithsonian.

Figure 68. The HP-41CV on board the Space Shuttle. The photo shows Astronaut Sally Ride aboard the Space Shuttle *Challenger* in June 1983. The calculator that was later donated to the Smithsonian is on the left of the three floating to her right. While in space, astronauts used it to calculate their orbital position, to process experimental data, and as a programmable alarm clock. Most of the time during a mission, each astronaut carried a calculator in a pocket of his or her flight suit. NASA photo.

Personal Computers

With the benefit of hindsight, it was inevitable that someone, somewhere, would have invented a personal computer by taking an inexpensive microprocessor and designing a simple computer around it. The truth is more complex, and historians have not yet fully sorted it out. That is because understanding the invention of the personal computer must include an understanding of the social as well as technical components of a computer that is "personal." The personal computer not only had to satisfy the technical and economic requirements of low cost and sufficient computing power, it also had to be perceived by its owners as a personal device, just as the automobile was perceived as a personal transport device 75 years ago.

In the early 1970s engineers within Digital Equipment Corporation, Hewlett-Packard, and IBM proposed to build and market an inexpensive, general-purpose personal computer. But their managers each in turn rejected their proposals, all for the same reason: the projected market was too small. Meanwhile, radio and electronics hobbyist magazines were publishing articles on how to build sophisticated digital devices using the chips then becoming available at low prices. By 1973, the market that the personal computer eventually filled was being nibbled at from above, by inexpensive minicomputers, and from below, by pocket calculators and hobbyists' kits.

In the spring of 1974 the California firm of Intel introduced its 8080 microprocessor, an integrated circuit on which were placed most of the circuits for a general-purpose computer. Based on a concept developed by Intel engineer Marcian "Ted" Hoff, the 8080 processed data in 8-bit words and could directly address up to 64,000 words of memory. It was not the first microprocessor on the market, but it was the first to have enough power to form the basis of a computer with general capabilities. Microprocessors like the 8080 ignited the personal computer phenomenon; what is often forgotten is that they are also incorporated into cash registers, calculators, teaching machines, kitchen appliances, automobile engines, power tools—in short, almost every machine that could benefit

One center of activity in modern computing is in the Santa Clara Valley, a former agricultural region south of Stanford University. Don Hoeffler, a journalist covering the region for Electronic News, *called it "Silicon Valley" in a series of articles in January 1971. The name stuck.*

from a measure of automatic control. Those applications were what Hoff and his co-workers at Intel probably had in mind, and the social impact of these so-called "smart" machines has been as great as, though less visible than, the impact of microprocessor-based personal computers.

This chapter looks at the evolution of the personal computer from its origin as a hobbyist phenomenon to a central piece of equipment used in most offices today. It begins with the Altair, whose introduction in 1975 sparked the phenomenon, and the IMSAI, similar to the Altair and introduced about a year later. The shift from the hobbyist to the consumer market is represented by the TRS-80, from Radio Shack, and the famous Apple II. The Osborne computer illustrates the constant trend not only toward smaller size and portability, but also toward providing complete systems, including software, to customers who otherwise did not wish to be involved in the details of assembling a useful system. The IBM Personal Computer, introduced in 1981, represents a further transition, this time to the business and office environment. The chapter ends with two computers that represented innovative designs: the Tandy Radio Shack Model 100 "Laptop," and the Apple Macintosh, with its graphics-based system that allowed users to control the machine without learning a complex computer language.

References: Braun and Macdonald (1982), Mims (1985), Noyce and Hoff (1981), Warren (1977).

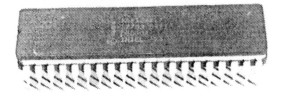

Figure 69. Intel 8080A microprocessor (1974), from the collections of the National Museum of American History. The Intel 8080 was used in the Altair and many other early personal computers. It incorporated about 5,000 transistors plus other circuits on a silicon chip, which was encapsulated in a black epoxy "Dual In-line Package" (or DIP), from which forty pins protruded to make external electrical connections. The chip itself is much smaller than the package shown here: it measures only about 1/4 in. square (6 mm × 6 mm). Intel continued the 80 series with a line of similar chips that had greater processing speed and memory capacity. These later chips—the 8086, '286, '386, and so on—are the most widely used in personal computers. Dimensions: 2 1/8 × 5/8 × 3/8 in. (5.3 × 1.5 × 1 cm). Photo by Rick Vargas, Smithsonian.

Not long after Intel introduced its 8080 chip, a small firm in Albuquerque, New Mexico, named MITS (Micro Instrumentation and Telemetry Systems) announced a computer kit called the Altair, which met the social as well as technical requirements for a personal machine. MITS succeeded where other, more established firms had failed, and it was their machine that inaugurated the personal computer age. MITS got its start in computing in 1971, when it introduced an electronic calculator kit. Several thousand sold before 1974, when the sharp reduction in calculator prices drove the company out of that market.

H. Edward Roberts, the Florida-born former U.S. Air Force officer who headed MITS, decided to design a small, affordable computer around the Intel 8080. His daughter named the new machine after the star Altair. It was the first microcomputer to sell in large numbers—thousands were sold, although for reasons that will be explained below, not all of them were used to do very much. In January 1975, a photograph of the Altair appeared on the cover of the magazine *Popular Electronics*. The caption read "World's First Minicomputer Kit to Rival Commercial Models." According to the magazine, the machine sold as a kit for $395 and assembled for $498. Roberts had hoped to break even by selling 200 Altairs. Within three months he had a backlog of 4000 orders.

The kit offered by MITS represented the minimum configuration of circuits that one could legitimately call a "computer." It had little internal and no external memory, no printer, and no keyboard or other input device. An Altair fitted out with those items might cost $4000—the equivalent to the cheapest PDP-8 minicomputer, a reliable and established performer. Most purchasers found the kit was difficult to assemble, unless they had experience with digital electronics and a workbench fitted out with sophisticated test equipment. And even if one assembled the kit correctly it was sometimes difficult to get the Altair to operate reliably.

But hobbyists were tolerant. In fact, their tolerance and enthusiasm were the key to the launching of the personal computer. Those who bought the Altair did so not because they had a specific computing job to do, but because they understood the potential of owning a general-purpose, stored-program computer. They understood the social as well as technical implications of the word "personal," and were willing to put up with the difficulties of bringing personal computers into existence. The personal computer's social appeal was that its owner could do as he or she wished with it.

Figure 70. MITS Altair 8800 (1975). The designation "8800" referred to the fact that the computer used an Intel 8080 chip. Hobbyists who successfully put together their Altairs ended up with a blue, box-shaped machine that measured 17 ×18 × 7in. (43.2 × 45.7 × 17.7 cm). To enter programs or data, one set the toggle switches on the front. There was no keyboard, video terminal or paper tape reader. All programming was in the machine code of binary digits. The first Altairs came with only 256 bytes of memory; they also lacked output devices such as printers. Results of a program were indicated by the pattern of flashing lights on the front panel. But the Altair did have many empty slots inside, into which additional circuit boards could easily be inserted. The Altair shown here is from the National Museum of American History Collections and was donated to the museum by Forrest Mims, one of the founders of MITS. Photo by Laurie Minor, Smithsonian.

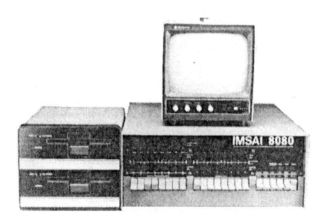

Figure 71. IMSAI (1976). The IMSAI, from IMSAI Manufacturing of San Leandro, California, appeared a year after the Altair and followed that computer's design closely. It used an Intel 8080 microprocessor and the S-100 bus. Like most of the early personal computers, it had an array of switches on the front panel for entering data and programs one bit at a time. The IMSAI's main distinction was that it had a rugged power supply, and for that reason it was more popular among hobbyists than the Altair. However IMSAI's attempt to break out of the hobbyist market and into business sales faltered, and the company went bankrupt in 1979. The computer shown here, from the collections of the National Museum of American History, was built by its donor, Kenneth S. Widelitz. He used it with a disc drive manufactured by Micropolis and a Sanyo monitor. The computer alone measures 17⅜ × 19⅕ × 7⅛ in. (44 × 50 × 18 cm). Photo by Eric Long, Smithsonian.

Enthusiasm for the Altair and other personal computers spawned computer hobbyist clubs, computer stores, newsletters, magazines, and conventions. By 1977 a host of companies, large and small, were producing microcomputers for a mass market. This phenomenon was abetted by a design decision by Roberts to make the Altair an "open" machine—it passed data along a channel called a bus, whose specifications were not kept secret or proprietary. That way both MITS and other companies could add memory cards, cards to control a printer, or other devices as long as they adhered to the published standard. That concept, pioneered by minicomputer manufacturers, would become the hallmark of the most successful personal computers. Most of these competitive personal computers followed the basic MITS design of using an 8080 microprocessor and its internal bus (called the "S-100," since it specified 100 signal paths). That same year, MITS's stockholders sold out to the Pertec Computer Corporation; by then the Altair had already been surpassed by several competitors.

Some early manufacturers of microcomputers, such as IMSAI, tried to interest businesses in their products. But with their reliability problems and with little business-oriented software, personal computers were still the domain of hobbyists. The Heath Company of Benton Harbor, Michigan, long known to amateur radio operators and electronics hobbyists, for example, brought out a $375 computer kit in the summer of 1977. Like the Altair and IMSAI, the Heath H-8 was based on the Intel 8080 processor, and was programmed in machine language (a slight improvement over the Altair lay in the fact that it accepted numbers in base-8, or Octal, instead of base-2, or binary). It was well regarded by hobbyists but found little acceptance beyond them. (The Zenith Corporation, a company with experience in consumer electronics, eventually bought Heath's computer division and turned it into a successful product line.) The use of personal computers in stores and offices would only expand with the introduction of accounting and word-processing software, the development of microcomputer networks, and the expansion of available memory.

References: Freiberger and Swaine (1984), Mims (1985), Roberts and Yates (1975).

Personal Computers: The Second Wave

Among the many personal computers marketed in 1977 were three that offered fairly complete systems that a person without a technical background could set up and use: the TRS-80 from the consumer giant Tandy Radio Shack, the PET from Commodore, and the Apple II, from the tiny Apple Computer Company of Cupertino, California. All three sold well. Their success indicated that there was a market beyond that of hobbyists, if one offered a product that did not require the equivalent of a degree in electrical engineering to assemble, test, and troubleshoot it.

"The Personal Computer will fall flat on its face in business."
—Ken Olsen, CEO of Digital Equipment Corporation, ca 1980; quoted in Rifkin and Harrar (1988, p. 199).

Don French, a buyer for the consumer electronics chain Tandy Radio Shack, was convinced that the company ought to offer a personal computer. Initially Radio Shack, which had experienced phenomenal growth selling audio equipment and citizen's band radios in its chain of stores across the country, was skeptical: computers were difficult to set up and use, and Radio Shack's customers were typically interested in low prices and ease of use, not in the underlying technology. Although Radio Shack stores did sell wires, switches, and circuit parts for the hobbyist, its main customers neither knew nor cared much about what went on inside the "black boxes" they bought. Eventually the company relented and in the summer of 1977 introduced the TRS-80, at a base price of only $400. It was indeed a complete machine, although the base model had only 4K bytes of memory and could not handle lowercase letters. One could expand its storage and input/output by purchasing an Expansion Interface at additional cost. But it did work as advertised, and the TRS-80 easily met Tandy's sales projections. The company soon introduced advanced models with more internal memory and disk drives instead of cassettes for entering programs.

Of the three computers introduced that summer, the Apple II soon pulled away from the rest. Despite a basic price of $1200, much more than what other companies were charging for their products, the Apple II not only outsold the others, its success also came to symbolize the personal computer phenomenon. In explaining its success, many have pointed to its name, its attractive packaging, and the company's astute management. The name Apple was a pleasant contrast to the pseudotechnical jargon that prevailed among mainframe manufacturers. And while the company was driven by the vision of Steven Jobs and the technical skills of Steve Wozniak, it also enjoyed the prudent and experienced management of Mike Markkula, who had retired (while in his mid-thirties) after a successful career at Intel and Fairchild. In addition, Jobs had persuaded Regis McKenna, a talented and successful public relations and advertising executive, to take on Apple as a client.

There were technical reasons for the Apple's success as

Figure 72. Tandy Radio Shack TRS-80. The monitor, which was an ordinary television set without a tuner, rests on top of the Expansion Interface. The TRS-80 used the Zilog Z-80 microprocessor, which was compatible with the Intel 8080 but slightly more powerful. The computer shown here is from the collections of the National Museum of American History. The computer and disk drives fit in a case which measures 29 × 24 × 8⅝ in. (74 cm × 61 × 22 cm). Photo by Eric Long, Smithsonian.

Figure 73. Apple Computer Company Apple II (1977). Unlike most of the hobbyist computers, the Apple II was housed in an attractive beige plastic case, with a full-sized and comfortable keyboard integral to the machine. The disk drive and television monitor were separate. From the National Museum of American History Collections. Dimensions of the processor and keyboard: 15 × 17 × 4 in. (38.1 × 43.2 × 10.2 cm). The machine shown here was owned by the spouse of a curator, who used it for museum work before donating it to the Museum of American History. Photo by Dane Penland, Smithsonian.

well. It had an open architecture like the Altair. It sup-
ported color graphics that made it suitable for games—
something few other computers at any price could do.
Steve Wozniak designed a fast and elegant driver to interface the Apple II with a floppy disk drive. The floppy had
been invented a decade earlier as an inexpensive storage
device for mainframe system software, but it soon found a
place as a cost-effective memory device for minicomputers
and then, with Apple's initiative, personal computers.
Apple's floppy drive removed the last technical obstacle
that had held the personal computer back. The speed of
the disk drive balanced well with the Apple's internal processing speeds, and it was more reliable than paper tapes
and modified audio cassette recorders, which only the
most dedicated hobbyists had the patience to use. With
floppy disks the personal computer found a wider market.
By the end of 1980 over 120,000 Apple IIs had been sold.

References: Augarten (1984), Freiberger and Swaine (1984).

Osborne Transportable

The success of the Apple II demonstrated that personal
computers were serious machines of use to more than just
hobbyists. But using one still required some knowledge of
electronics, at the very least to plug in and test the various
components. Obtaining the necessary software, without
which the computer was useless, could also be daunting. A
series of developments beginning around 1980 helped
change the computer into an "appliance." That further
broadened the market.

Adam Osborne, an engineer who had taken on a second career writing documentation for computers, surveyed the booming and chaotic personal-computer
phenomenon and decided to enter the fray with a product
of his own. He envisioned a compact appliance, light
enough to be carried as luggage and small enough to fit
under an airline seat. It would be just cheap enough to be
purchased with one's credit card, thus encouraging
impulse sales (in those days one typically had a limit of
$2000, so Osborne priced his machine at $1795). For that
price one would get everything needed to begin computing right away: system software as well as programs for
word processing and a database. That concept was revolutionary in the climate of the day, where the purchaser had
to assemble a computer system out of a myriad of different pieces, hoping they would fit, and only then begin
thinking of where to find software that would do a certain
job. When his machine was announced at that price, mag-

Figure 74. Osborne computer. The Osborne was about the size of a portable sewing machine. The bottom cover detached and folded out to become the keyboard, and at the same time it revealed the 5 in. (12.7 cm) screen flanked by two floppy disk drives. The screen was too small to show a full 80 columns of text at a time, so it showed a "window" into the full screen. Despite these deficiencies, it was indeed what Osborne wanted: something that provided the basics, and nothing more. From the National Museum of American History Collections. Dimensions: 113 × 20 × 14 in. (32.5 × 50 × 36.5 cm); weight about 28 pounds (13 kg). Photo by Eric Long, Smithsonian.

azine reviewers noted that one would have to pay more than $2000 to buy such software alone, at the retail prices then current. Osborne was able to negotiate much lower prices from software vendors, in part by promising high-volume sales, in part because the software he selected, such as the CP/M operating system, was already somewhat obsolete.

Osborne enlisted the help of Lee Felsenstein, whom he called an "unrepentant Berkeley radical," to design the hardware, while Osborne himself went about negotiating for low-cost access to the software he knew the machine had to have. In March 1981 he announced the Osborne computer. It was an instant success and the company grew fast. Osborne later named the phenomenon "hyper-growth": growth too fast for a company's own good. By late 1983 the company was bankrupt. It had made a number of mistakes, nearly all related to its inability to manage such a fast pace. Competitors, especially Kaypro, were quick to bring out machines similar to the Osborne but with better disk drives, a more rugged case, and a monitor that displayed a full screen of text. The Osborne computer was cheap because it used an outmoded, 8-bit micro-processor and operating system; what the company had not anticipated was how quickly the IBM PC, which used a 16-bit processor and the MS-DOS operating system, would make those choices obsolete. Although Osborne had been working on a 16-bit version that was compatible with the IBM PC, he could not get it to market soon enough to stave off bankruptcy and collapse. Other companies, especially Compaq of Houston, Texas, took his idea and managed to survive "hypergrowth" without crashing. But it was Osborne who established the category of "portable" computer, while his concept of selling an appliance that one simply plugged in and used further broadened the market.

Reference: Osborne and Dvorak (1984)

During the early 1970s, IBM engineers in California developed a portable machine called the SCAMP for demonstrating computer languages. That led to a commercial product called the IBM 5100, intended for business use. The IBM 5100 cost considerably more than computers like the Altair and did not sell widely. By the summer of 1980, the success of the Apple II and other personal computers persuaded IBM to enter this market and to enter it quickly. Philip Don Estridge and a small team of employees at an IBM facility in Boca Raton, Florida, developed a computer that adopted an open design such as was used in the Altair and Apple II. That represented a major departure for IBM, which had a long tradition of designing its products to make it difficult for competitors to add to or modify them.

In designing the computer, IBM also proved unusually open in its use of the products of other companies. They subcontracted for many parts, including the microprocessor, the disk drives and the printer. A crucial decision was to use Intel's new 8088 microprocessor, which handled

Figure 75. An early IBM PC. The basic PC consisted of the processor (19.5 × 16 × 5.5 in.; 49.5 × 40.6 × 14 cm), monitor (15 ×15 × 11 in.; 38.1 × 38.1 × 28 cm) and keyboard. Two floppy disk drives are built in to the processor chassis. IBM also introduced a simple printer with the system. Parts of the system were priced separately, so the cost ran from about $1,595 upward. The computer shown here is on exhibit at the National Museum of American History. Photo by Eric Long, Smithsonian.

data in 16-bit words, instead of the 8-bit microprocessors nearly every other personal computer used. Much of the software, including the operating system, also came from outside sources. IBM's selection of Microsoft Corporation to provide the PC's operating system was a key event that propelled that company into the ranks of one of the world's largest corporations. Abandoning its traditional reliance on an in-house sales force, IBM sold the computer through commercial outlets. The machine was a great success, selling in the millions, and it set a standard for the microcomputer industry. Numerous imitators designed "clones" that performed like the IBM PC. Others wrote software for use with its operating system, and publications for users flourished.

References: Anonymous (1986), Freiberger and Swaine (1984), Levering, Katz, and Moskowitz (1984).

TRS-80 Model 100

Computers like the Osborne were portable, but weighing over 25 pounds, they were hardly easy to carry around. One magazine ad showed a petite executive dashing to an airport gate with an Osborne computer comfortably in her hand, but in Adam Osborne's later account of his company, he confessed that the photograph was elaborately staged to hide the actual weight of the machine. Nonetheless, the popularity of these computers revealed a substantial demand for portability. Radio Shack, which had brought out its successful TRS-80 in 1977, contracted with the Japanese company Kyoto Ceramics (Kyocera) to produce a machine that was much more portable. Introduced in the summer of 1983, the Model 100 was about the size of a three-ring notebook and weighed only 4 pounds. Although small, it still had a full-sized keyboard that anyone used to an electric typewriter would feel comfortable with. Like the Osborne, it came with simple but useful software built in—the Basic programming language, a simple word processor, and a filing program. This software was written by William Gates, founder and chairman of Microsoft Corporation.

The Model 100 also contained a built-in modem and communications software that allowed one to transfer files to another computer over the telephone. The machine thus compromised on some features, but on others, especially the keyboard, it did not. The Model 100 was especially popular with journalists, who could write a story in the field and file it from any nearby telephone booth. Its success spawned still another class of computer, the "laptop," which has since become one of the most popular.

Reference: Lammers (1989).

Figure 76. Tandy Radio Shack TRS-80, Model 100. The dimensions are 8.5 ×12 × 2 in. (21.5 cm × 30.5 × 5 cm); weight is 4 pounds (1.8 kg). The Model 100 had no disk drives and used a small liquid-crystal display instead of the video terminal the other portables used. That made it extremely compact and allowed the machine to be run off four penlight batteries, further reducing size and weight. It used an 80C85 processor, a low-power version of the ones used by the first-generation personal computers like the Altair. For a base price of $800, one got 8 kilobytes of memory. An ordinary audio cassette recorder was used to store programs and data; later on, third-party vendors supplied more internal memory capacity and external disk drives. The computer shown here is from the collections of the National Air and Space Museum and was used by one of its curators. Photo: Mark Avino, Smithsonian.

In 1979 Apple Computer Company was still enjoying brisk sales of its Apple II, but the fast-growing company was having trouble with a follow-on to that product. They had two products under development, the Apple III and the Lisa, but Steven Jobs, a co-founder of the company, was not happy with the progress or design of either.

That year he visited the laboratories of Xerox's Palo Alto Research Center (PARC), where he saw a computer called the Alto and the innovative software and graphics being developed with it. The Alto reflected the ideas of a number of researchers, especially those of Douglas Engelbart, who in the 1950s worked at the Stanford Research Institute on ways in which computers might be used to "augment human intellect," in his words. With funds from military agencies of the U.S. government, Engelbart and his colleagues sought to ease communication between computer users and their machines. They introduced individual computer monitors on which data could be modified both by typing in text and by moving an electronic pointer, which they named a "mouse."

When the U.S. reduced defense spending toward the end of the Vietnam War, funds for Engelbart's laboratory were sharply curtailed. Several of his colleagues went to work nearby at the Xerox PARC, where they applied some of Engelbart's ideas to the Alto. Xerox did have its own plans for commercializing the Alto, but it also had been an early investor in the Apple Computer Company, and it saw no harm in allowing a representative from a company a fraction its size to visit the Palo Alto labs.

Jobs felt that the approach being taken by Xerox showed the direction all personal computers would take. He redirected the development of the Lisa to incorporate those features, but when introduced in 1983, its price of around $10,000 placed it out of the "personal" market that Jobs wanted to attain. Jobs began developing a new product that would have the Alto's features but which would cost less than $1,000. When finally introduced as the Macintosh in 1984, it cost over twice that, but it did embody the Xerox PARC approach to computing in an elegant way.

Jobs believed that the Macintosh would carry on the tradition begun by the first wave of personal computers and bring computing power to the individual, on the individual's terms, free of any centralized control whether corporate or government. Apple claimed that the computer's design and use of graphics made it as easy to use as any other household appliance—that one could take it out of the box, plug it in, and immediately begin using it.

That claim was based on the Macintosh's system software, patterned after that developed for the Xerox Alto: icons to represent files and programs, overlapping "windows" displaying a user's work, and a mouse—all available in a low-cost, compact computer for the first time. Researchers at Xerox's PARC reflected the legacy of the U.S Defense Department's computing programs: an emphasis on technical innovation and ease of use for the soldier in the field, but also high cost, exotic hardware, and no concern for production or sales to a consumer market. Apple Computer Corporation grew from a core of hobbyists, who appreciated an elegant design and low cost, but who cared less about whether it was easy for someone who is not an electronics enthusiast to use a computer. The Macintosh represented a meeting of the two cultures, and it established an alternative to the IBM PC and its copies. In time Apple's competitors would copy the concepts employed in the Macintosh as well.

References: Rose (1989).

Figure 77. Apple Macintosh (1984). The Macintosh was based around the Motorola 68000 processor, and initially came with 128 thousand bytes (128 K) of memory and one disk drive. The demands that the graphics placed on memory soon became evident, and a 512 K version was added soon after, while many users found the need to purchase a second, external disk drive. Unlike the Apple II and the IBM PC, users were not supposed to open the machine up to make any modifications; there were no internal slots for adding circuits anyway. The machine used compact and rugged 3.5 in. disks instead of the 5.25 in. disks most other personal computers used, and it had a small but readable black and white screen. The result was an attractive computer that was a third the size of the IBM PC and that could easily fit on the most crowded desk. Dimensions (less keyboard): 10 × 14 ×11 in. (25.5 × 35.5 × 28 cm). The machine shown here was one of the first off the production line; it was given to the National Museum of American History as a gift from Apple Computer Corporation. Photo by Dane Penland, Smithsonian.

Networks, Supercomputers, and Workstations, 1976–1985

In the 1980s a number of companies introduced machines that established a new class: the "personal workstation." Typically these computers were intended for use by a single individual, and came with interactive graphics and networking capability. Superficially they resembled personal computers, but they had more processing speed and graphics ability and were intended from the start to be networked. As such, they were part of a distributed computing system that includes other classes of machines, including mainframes, minicomputers, and high-performance "supercomputers." Supercomputers, which also emerged at this time, are optimized to perform complex scientific calculations at high speeds. They are expensive to operate and maintain, but they allow researchers to gain an understanding of complex natural phenomena that otherwise would be impossible to uncover.

The first customers for workstations were in aerospace and other technically sophisticated firms, where engineers used the machines' graphics capabilities for computer-aided design (CAD). In these applications it is critical that the computers be networked, as engineering design requires constant communication and sharing of data among many members of a large team. The savings in time that formerly went into the production of complex, hand-drawn blueprints and engineering drawings more than offset the high costs of these machines. Later, as their cost dropped below $20,000, they found other users. For example, workstations became common among Wall Street traders in commodities, stock futures, and foreign currencies. These financial wizards—their colleagues sometimes call them "rocket scientists"—employ complex programs that show the latest financial information from markets around the world, each displayed in a different window on the screen. With such programs, a trader can spot a difference of a few pennies in the price of a commodity at different markets, and execute a trade based on that difference in an instant.

Workstations, networks, and supercomputers are all rapidly evolving, and there is little consensus how or when the technology will settle. For that reason we hesitate to call these machines "landmarks," even though they may seem in common use in today's office, home, or laboratory. Events of the next few years might reveal that what today seems like the main avenue of development was in fact a dead end. The following chapter therefore presents only a modest selection of machines that cover the range of the topic. It begins with the Xerox Alto, a machine that introduced many of the features common to modern personal workstations. An early CRAY-1 illustrates the supercomputer class of machines; these computers, though still exotic and expensive, nevertheless incorporate features that over time may become common in lower-priced devices. One of the first commercially successful workstations, from SUN Microsystems, is described, and the chapter ends with a more recent SUN workstation incorporating what the computer industry calls "RISC" architecture (for "Reduced Instruction Set Computer"). Industry analysts are enthusiastic in their assertion that RISC machines herald a new era in computation. But only time will tell whether future generations will recognize them as "landmarks" as today we recognize the ENIAC, the Whirlwind, the Ritty cash register, or the Scheutz difference engine.

References: Goldberg (1988), Patterson (1985).

XEROX Alto

Xerox PARC, the Xerox Corporation's research center located in Palo Alto, California, was the birthplace of the workstation. The Alto, the machine they developed in 1973 that influenced Apple's products, had additional features not used in the Apple Macintosh. In particular the Alto's designers developed a networking scheme, called Ethernet, which linked the machines at PARC and allowed them to share data, programs, and resources among each other. That concept reversed the conventional wisdom, which was to have all the computing power residing in a central, large mainframe, served on a time-shared basis by "dumb" terminals that had little or no processing power or storage in them. With the Alto, the network itself became part of the computer's architecture.

By 1979, nearly 1,000 Altos were in use, mainly within Xerox Corporation. The company introduced a commercial version of the machine, called the Star, in 1981. However, at $16,000 per machine, this proved too expensive to generate large sales. The Alto's concept of distributed computing through a local area network did not carry over into the personal computers like the IBM PC or even the Macintosh. The microprocessors that the early personal computers used could not handle the task of networking, and PC manufacturers wanted to keep costs low.

Figure 78. Xerox Alto. Each Alto was designed for a single user, and contained a keyboard, mouse, video monitor, and a processing unit that fit under a desk. The Alto monitor featured a high-resolution screen split into several sections or windows, with a menu of computer commands. To select a command from the menu, users moved the mouse to position a pointer over the desired item, and then pressed a button. From the National Museum of American History Collections. The display, keyboard, and mouse measure, overall, 18½ × 16 × 21 in. (47 × 40.5 × 53 cm). The processor measures 27¼ × 28 × 22½ in. (70.5 × 71 × 57 cm). Photo by Laurie Minor, Smithsonian.

Likewise, the operating system most personal computers used, Microsoft's MS-DOS, was ill suited for networking. Practical networking demanded both a better processor and more sophisticated system software.

Reference: Johnson et al. (1989).

While Xerox engineers were designing personal systems, others were designing large computers that would push performance beyond existing levels. From about 1965 to 1990, the most successful designer of high-performance computers was the modest, plain-spoken Seymour Cray. Born in Chippewa Falls, Wisconsin, in 1925, Cray studied electrical engineering and applied mathematics at the University of Minnesota in Minneapolis. After receiving a Masters degree in 1951, he went to work for Engineering Research Associates (ERA, later part of Univac). In 1957 Cray left Univac and helped found Control Data Corporation, where he was responsible for design and development of computers that broke through existing boundaries in processing speeds and performance. It was with the introduction of these machines—the CDC 6600 and 7600—that the term "supercomputer" came into use. The CDC machines were the first to be built in large numbers and successfully marketed to a variety of customers.

In 1972, Cray left CDC, feeling that a smaller organization was better suited to his goal of building the world's fastest computers. He founded Cray Research, Inc., and established a laboratory near his home in Chippewa Falls. Four years later the company announced its first product, the CRAY-1. This computer used many of the design techniques Cray used in the CDC machines, but in adddition it achieved high performance by its ability to perform arithmetic simultaneously on all of the numbers in a vector (an array of numbers)—most other computers required a separate instruction for each number. About 85 copies of the CRAY-1 sold at a base price of $5 million. Cray Research and a host of other firms have since developed supercomputers with similar or better performance. The development of supercomputers continues to be a dynamic field where new concepts in computer design are explored, especially those that seek to process large arrays of data in parallel. Because of their high cost, however, sales of supercomputers are likely to remain small, although some of the ideas they embody, like parallel processing, may find their way into the mass market. One of the more interesting developments in workstations would be to provide supercomputer capabilities at lower cost. Presently, however, one must still be prepared to spend a lot of money to get this performance.

Reference: Siewiorek, Bell, and Newell (1982).

Figure 79. CRAY-1 computer, processor. The CRAY-1 shown is #14, from the National Center for Atmospheric Research in Boulder, Colorado. It was retired in 1986 and donated to the Smithsonian by Cray Research, and it is now on exhibit at the National Air and Space Museum. The computer is deceptively small, with the circuit boards arranged in a three-quarter circle (the opening in the circle allows a person to service the machine from its inside, if necessary.) Power supplies and cooling equipment are in a ring below each circuit column, with wires connecting the circuit boards to one another on the inside of the circle. The circular shape minimizes the distance, and therefore the delay time, from one circuit board to another. Likewise the hand-soldered wires carry signals much faster than printed circuit paths. The cooling system and power supplies at the bottom of the machine are located close by, to minimize voltage drops. Its memory uses integrated circuits and holds one million words. The CRAY-1 has no operator's console; in normal use it is connected to a minicomputer or a network of workstations, from which it is controlled. Dimensions: 6 feet high, 7 feet in diameter (1.8 m × 2.1 m). Photo by Carolyn Russo, Smithsonian.

Figure 80. A typical CRAY-1 installation, showing the array of disk and tape drives used to support the processing unit. Photo by Cray Research, Inc.

SUN Workstation

By the mid-1980s powerful microprocessors appeared that could handle networking, the most popular being the Motorola 68000 family. An operating system, with more capabilities than MS-DOS, also gained commercial acceptance after years of low-key development and use in selected research environments. That system was UNIX. UNIX had one more desirable feature: low cost. Since UNIX was developed at AT&T's Bell Laboratories, at a time when AT&T was a regulated monopoly not permitted to enter the computer business, AT&T licensed the operating system at a nominal cost to anyone who wanted it. That helped spread UNIX among university computing environments, where it gained a number of devoted followers.

By the mid-1980s there was a glut of these workstations available on the market—so many that the trade journals coined the acronym "JAWS," meaning "just another workstation." But a few of them stood out and began to develop a substantial market. Among these were machines sold by SUN Microsystems, Inc., of Mountain View, California. In May 1982 they introduced their first workstation, based on the Motorola processor and UNIX. Its high performance, low cost, and adherence to established standards of operating systems and internal connections firmly established SUN as a leading workstation company.

Reference: Hall and Barry (1990).

Figure 81. SUN-2 Workstation (1985). The SUN used a Motorola 68000 processor and came with 1 megabyte of memory. Like the Alto, its display was "bitmapped" (each picture element, or pixel, was separately controllable). Data were displayed on the screen in overlapping tiles or "windows," and it used a mouse to select items on the screen. An Ethernet network connection was standard, as was an internal architecture (Multibus) that offered a standardized connection to other manufacturers' input and output devices. The operating system was Berkeley's version of UNIX, again a standard widely known and used in the academic community. The machine shown here, a SUN-2, was a slightly more advanced version of the company's first workstation. It is on exhibit at the National Museum of American History. Dimensions: 17⅞ × 24 × 19⅜ in. (45.5 × 61 × 49.2 cm). Photo by Richard Strauss, Smithsonian.

In the mid-1980s, advances in chip technology led a number of designers to rethink the assumptions that lay behind the designs of existing machines, from PCs to mainframes and even supercomputers. Specifically, they saw that high-speed memory chips made it practical to design much faster processors by simplifying and reducing the number of instructions they could execute. These "Reduced Instruction Set Computers" (RISC) could execute their instructions much faster than computers having a complex instruction set; the higher memory speeds compensated for the lack of complex instructions. This design was a clear alternative to the dominant architectures then popular, such as those found in the IBM mainframes, the VAX, and most personal computers. SUN, Hewlett-Packard, and IBM (where key concepts of RISC designs were first worked out) each introduced a RISC workstation after 1987, and since then RISC architectures have gained mainstream acceptance. They point toward a set of common architectures for all computers in the coming decade.

Reference: Hall and Barry (1990).

Figure 82. SUN SPARC workstation, 1992, that uses a reduced-instruction-set or "RISC" architecture. Bruce Campbell, a researcher at the Smithsonian's Center for Earth and Planetary Studies, is using it to process an image of the surface of Venus taken by the Magellan space probe. The computer is the thin box on which the monitor rests: it measures only 16 ×16 × 3 in. (41 × 41 × 8 cm). Its users call it a "pizza box" computer because of its shape. Photo by Carolyn Russo, Smithsonian.

Epilogue

The popular notion of the computer is that it is an invention of the late 1940s. This chronicle of landmarks shows that, although technological innovation in the 1940s was remarkable, many characteristics of modern computing have a long ancestry. Jacquard built a machine to automate the production of graphical patterns on cloth; the modern workstation employs powerful graphics software to make complex mathematical relationships more understandable to its users. For centuries, an Asian merchant might have carried a small abacus to assist in reckoning; a seventeenth century European might carry a set of Napier's "bones" in his pocket. Today's engineer continues that practice with a Hewlett-Packard calculator in his or her pocket. The Dudley Observatory bought one of Scheutz's elaborate and costly difference engines to do astronomical work; today's astrophysicists rely on supercomputers like the CRAY-1 and its descendants. Early twentieth century businesses like railroads and electric utilities embraced Herman Hollerith's punched-card equipment to keep from being swamped by quantities of data their businesses generated; the modern mainframe computer, like the descendants of the IBM System/360, does exactly the same job. The computer "revolution" is less sudden than its proponents would have us believe.

During the past four centuries, people have designed and sold computing devices of increasing speed and complexity. Often they were introduced as expensive, one-of-a-kind instruments. These were then standardized and eventually mass-produced. Specially made adding machines like those of Pascal and Lepine were followed in the nineteenth century by commercial products like the Thomas arithmometer and then the mass-produced Comptometer, Burroughs adding machine, and Brunsviga calculating machines. Likewise, pioneering mainframe computers like the IAS were forerunners of the commercially produced UNIVAC I and IBM 701. These, in turn, established a precedent for more widely sold products like the IBM 650. Desktop electronic calculators were produced both as kits and in more standard commercial form. They soon were replaced by cheaper, faster, mass-produced handheld calculators. The hobbyist's home computer also paved a similar path, to the more powerful personal computer of a standard design that only slowly evolves.

As calculating machines and then electronic calculators and computers became standard products, they not only became cheaper and more reliable, but also required less understanding from their users. Seventeenth century mathematicians like Blaise Pascal designed adding machines. At the end of the nineteenth century calculators from companies like Felt & Tarrant began to find their way into ordinary businesses. In the mid-twentieth century, mathematical physicists like John von Neumann described general principles of computer architecture, and mathematicians like Grace Hopper designed programming languages. As products developed, however, mechanically minded inventors and specialists in computer hardware and software increasingly dominated the design of computing devices. Moreover, users did not need to know mathematics and mechanics or, later, electronics and programming.

In recent years, computer technology has been incorporated into a wide range of consumer and industrial products. At the same time, computers have come to be used in word processing, electronic mail, industrial design, video games, and speech synthesis. Such applications are quite different from traditional computation or data processing. Even when digital computers are used to compute, the output may take surprising form. Digital devices are used to plot graphs and to produce images of planets, of the Earth, and of molecules. In all of these cases, digital technology gives an analog representation.

In the late nineteenth century, the United States challenged European dominance of the development of calculating machines. In the late twentieth century, Japan has challenged American preeminence in electronic computing. The full significance of national styles, policies, and legal systems in the history of computing is not yet well understood. Some have predicted that the computer will fundamentally alter power relationships within society, although evidence of this is not yet generally accepted.

Trends

In a business so technology-driven as computing, any attempt to predict the future is bound to fail. The rapid pace of innovation is likely to continue, with the future bringing surprises that no one can predict. A simple extrapolation of existing trends points to an even smaller or cheaper class of computers, perhaps one with all the features of a PC but small enough to wear on one's wrist.

But smaller size alone may not produce a qualitatively new class. For one, the size of the human hand and acuity of the human eye will always mean a need for keyboards and displays of a certain size, although voice and handwriting recognition, or other novel input/output methods, may make many of the reasons we use keyboards and screens unnecessary. It is more likely that the next class, if one does appear, will be novel and unexpected, as were the mini and personal computer.

The rise of personal workstations indicates a trend that may herald the end of patterns that have persisted for nearly four decades. Despite the advances in device technology, the von Neumann architecture, exemplified by the IAS machine, remained a constant standard of computer design. And with the introduction of the IBM System/360, the notion of software-compatible families of computers has likewise been universally accepted—the concept formed the basis of the success of the VAX and the Intel 8080-based personal computers, to name only two. Since the late 1960s the division of computers into classes, from super to mainframe, through mini to personal, has also persisted.

Personal workstations represent a different philosophy: that of defining the computer's architecture not in terms of what is on one's desk but in terms of the system to which it is networked. In such an architecture much of the computing power that one uses is a property of the network; the user neither knows nor cares what sorts of machines are connected to it. Such a network may include mainframes to handle large quantities of data, supercomputers optimized for complex scientific work, and minicomputers to handle switching and message routing. But all that is invisible to the user. Likewise, the systems on such a network will embrace a variety of architectures, including massively parallel, "non–von Neumann" designs that are optimized for certain types of processing (such as image processing or weather forecasting).

In such a network, software compatibility among families of machines will be of concern to those running it, but most users may never have to deal with that issue. Through graphical models like that pioneered by the Macintosh, users will see only those applications they need. These will interact smoothly with one another, with all translation and conversion of data formats, commands, and such done automatically and hidden from view. Such a scenario resembles the home telephone. Except for the push-button instead of a rotary dial, and perhaps also a few more buttons for other functions, most telephones look the same as they did forty years ago. But the telephone system has evolved by orders of magnitude since then. Direct long-distance dialing, international calling, digital instead of analog transmission—all that has radically transformed telephony since 1950. But the telephone companies, to their credit, carefully designed the system to shield that complexity from the consumer. That is as it should be, since most users wish only to talk to one another, not learn the intricacies of the latest communications technologies. So it may be with computing.

Many people in the computer industry hold this vision of networked computing as personal, easy to use, and ubiquitous as the telephone, but it is not clear how, or when, or even if, it will happen. To implement such a vision will require some new technology, although most of the necessary technical pieces—the chips, architectures, and communications devices—are in place. More than that, it will depend on governments and industries agreeing on standards, uniform regulations, and protocols. When it does, the "computer" as a separate entity will disappear, and with that, the final "landmark" will be attained.

Chronology

The following chronology gives a general outline of the order in which digital computing devices have been introduced and offers some information not included in the text. It hides as much as it reveals about the actual practice of computing, however, for several reasons. Inventions take place over a number of years. Napier's description of his rods was published in the year of his death, but he probably invented them earlier. Hollerith tabulating machines were first used in significant numbers at the time of the U.S. Census of 1890, but Hollerith had built earlier versions of his machine and would continue to improve it. In more recent times, designing and building computers often takes several years from the first plans to the first operation of the machine to its dedication or first commercial installations. It may take years or indeed centuries for an invention to be translated into successful commercial products. Pascal may have built an adding machine in 1642, but adding machines were not manufactured in large numbers until the late nineteenth and early twentieth centuries. Similarly, it took time to establish a market for computers from the 1940s onward. Finally, even when new technologies have been adopted, old ones endure. The abacus and mathematical tables had their roots in antiquity but continue to be used today. Some weavers still use Jacquard looms. Calculating machines probably sold most widely in the days of early electronic computers. Today, the introduction of new personal computers may set new standards of performance, but many people continue to work with older models that salesmen would deride as obsolete and old-fashioned. Meanwhile, the majority of the world's population has no access whatsoever to these products. To sum up, the computing technologies and techniques have not succeeded one another in a simple chronological order but rather overlap.

ca 450 B.C.
Stones used as counters by Greeks. This form of an abacus
was adopted by the Romans by about 50 B.C. and developed
into the medieval European counting board

1200 A.D.
Hindu-Arabic numerals introduced into Europe

1300
Abacus, using beads strung on wires mounted in a frame, in
use in China

1500
Quipu used extensively by Incas

1614
Logarithms described by John Napier

1617
Napier described his calculating rods, or "bones," in a book
published the year of his death

1623
Wilhelm Schickard described, in a letter to Johannes Kepler,
an adding mechanism that automatically carried a "1" to the
column to the left whenever a sum of a column was greater
than 9. First known description of an adding machine

1642
Blaise Pascal's adding machine: oldest surviving example of a
true adding machine with tens carry

1673
Gottfried Wilhelm Leibniz's calculator mechanized multiplication, using a stepped drum, as well as addition

1725
Lepine's adding machine built

1803
Jacquard began work on an automatic loom using punched
cards

1820
Charles Xavier Thomas's arithmometer

1822
Charles Babbage completed a model of the difference engine,
a device that linked adding and subtracting mechanisms to
one another to calculate the values of more complex mathematical functions

1834
Babbage turned from construction of the difference engine

(never completed) to a far more ambitious analytical engine: a machine that embodied in its design most of the features of a modern digital computer

1843
Ada Augusta, Countess of Lovelace, published a description of Babbage's analytical engine that incorporated many of the concepts of modern computer programming

1851
Victor Schilt exhibited a key-driven adding machine at the Crystal Palace Exposition in London

1853
Scheutz difference engine completed: the world's first printing calculator

1854
George Boole published Laws of Thought, leading to what eventually would be called Boolean algebra. His rules for manipulating logical (as opposed to purely numeric) expressions would later be adopted by computer designers as the basis for the electronic circuits or "logic" of computers

1879
James and John Ritty patented a cash register

1884
John H. Patterson and his associates acquired the Ritty patents and established National Cash Register Company (NCR)

1885
Dorr Felt constructed the "macaroni box" prototype for his key-driven adding machine

1890
Hollerith punched-card equipment employed in U.S. census

1891
William S. Burroughs began commercial manufacture of his printing adding machine

1893
"Millionaire" calculator introduced in Switzerland. It allowed direct multiplication by any digit and was used by government agencies and scientists, especially astronomers, well into the 20th century

1911
Charles Flint founded the Computing-Tabulating-Recording Company (C-T-R), which produced and sold Hollerith tabu-

lating equipment, time clocks, and other business machinery James Powers began manufacturing a punched-card system that competed with Hollerith's, and which operated mechanically rather than electrically. His machines eventually were made and sold by the Remington-Rand Corporation

1917–18
Aberdeen Proving Ground, at Aberdeen, Maryland, developed mathematical techniques for computing and printing firing tables for new types of advanced ordnance used in World War I

1918
Charles Kettering developed the "Kettering Bug": an unmanned flying bomb, guided by internal gyroscopes

1919
Early versions of the Enigma cipher machine built in Europe

1924
Thomas Watson, President of C-T-R, changed the company's name to International Business Machines Corporation

1928
IBM adopted the 80-column punched card, the standard for the next 50 years

1930
Vannevar Bush of MIT developed the differential analyzer, a large analog computer

1933
Totalisator machine installed at racetrack near Chicago

1935
U.S. Social Security Act passed

1936
Alan Turing, a British mathematician, published "On Computable Numbers . . .," a mathematical description of a "machine" that could in principle solve any mathematical problem that could be presented to it in symbolic form. Turing proved mathematically that it was possible to build a computer that was not restricted to solving only one problem or even one class of problems. His work offered a theoretical basis for modern computer software

1937
George Stibitz, a research mathematician at Bell Telephone Laboratories in New York, built a binary adder out of a few

light bulbs, batteries, and wire on his kitchen table. His "Model K" (for "kitchen") demonstrated the feasibility of mechanizing binary arithmetic

First Social Security benefit check, printed on an IBM punched card, is issued to Mrs. Ida Fuller, of Ludlow, Vermont

1938
Claude Shannon, of MIT, showed in theory what Stibitz had demonstrated with the "Model K": that the two-valued algebra developed by George Boole could be implemented electrically by telephone relays

Konrad Zuse, a German mechanical engineer, began building a mechanical computer in his parents's Berlin apartment. Independently of Shannon, he developed a form of symbolic logic to assist in the design of the binary circuits

1939
World's Fair in New York featured many exhibits showing the promise of technology. Among them are "Elektro," a robot man that exhibited simple intelligence

J.V. Atanasoff began work on an electronic computer at Iowa State University, Ames

George Stibitz and Samuel Williams of Bell Telephone Laboratories completed the Complex Number Computer (later known as the Bell Labs Model I). The machine used telephone relays and coded decimal numbers as groups of four binary digits (bits) each

1940
Stibitz demonstrated the Bell Labs Model I at Dartmouth College, with a terminal in New Hampshire and the Model I in New York. Twenty years later Dartmouth would become a center for time-sharing and remote use of electronic digital computers

1941
Within a few days of America's entry into World War II, Konrad Zuse demonstrated a working, programmable calculator to German military authorities. His "Z3" used surplus telephone relays and was programmed by holes punched into discarded 35mm movie film

1942
J. Presper Eckert and John Mauchly, of the University of Pennsylvania, propose an electronic version of the Bush differential analyzer for the Army, which would operate digitally instead of by analog means. The proposal led to the ENIAC

1943
Electromechanical Bombes built in Britain and U.S. to decipher German messages encrypted by Enigma

1944
First of several Colossus machines completed in Britain, using vacuum tubes instead of relay circuits, to decipher German messages

The ASCC, also known as the Harvard Mark I, was unveiled at Cruft Laboratory, Cambridge, Massachusetts

1945
ENIAC completed and tested at the Moore School of Electrical Engineering, University of Pennsylvania

Konrad Zuse completed the "Z4," a large electromechanical programmable machine, shortly before VE–day. Machine was dismantled and shipped from Berlin to a village in the Bavarian Alps, and eventually was installed at the Federal Technical Institute of Zurich, Switzerland

"First Draft of a Report on the EDVAC" written by John von Neumann. This 101-page mimeographed document summarized the discussions at the Moore School concerning the proposed successor to the ENIAC. Von Neumann's reputation as a world-class mathematician, as well as his description of the EDVAC in symbolic rather than engineering terms, helped win widespread acceptance of his design

1946
February: public unveiling of the ENIAC in Philadelphia

Summer: a series of lectures on the "Theory and Techniques for Design of Electronic Digital Computers" given at the Moore School in Philadelphia. The course led to widespread adoption of the EDVAC-type design, including stored programs, for nearly all subsequent computer development

December: the first of the two Bell Labs Model V computers completed (the second was built in 1947)

1947
December: point-contact transistor invented at Bell Labs

1948
Cybernetics, by Norbert Wiener, published. This widely read and influential book discussed some of the effects computers might have on society

Manchester "baby" prototype operated successfully. This small pilot version of a larger computer then being built at the University of Manchester in England is believed to be the first operable electronic digital computer that stored its programs internally

1949
May: EDSAC first operated in Cambridge, England. Built by Maurice Wilkes, who had attended the 1946 Moore School lectures, it is regarded as the first practical stored-program computer to operate in the world

BINAC (Binary Automatic Computer), built by Eckert and Mauchly, completed and shipped to Northrop Aircraft of Hawthorne, California; first stored-program computer in the United States to operate. It was never reliable enough to be put into routine service

1950
Bell Labs Model VI completed: last of the Bell Labs relay computers

SEAC (Standards Eastern Automatic Computer) completed at the National Bureau of Standards, Washington, D.C.; the first practical stored program computer to operate and be put into routine service in U.S.

ERA 1101 completed; stored-program computer built by alumni of wartime codebreaking projects in St. Paul, Minnesota. Beginnings of Twin Cities computer industry

1951
April: Whirlwind computer began operation

June: first UNIVAC I completed in Philadelphia and formally turned over to U.S. Census Bureau

1952
IAS computer first operated at the Institute for Advanced Study, Princeton

UNIVAC "Automatic Programming" systems developed: "A-0," "B-0" et al. These were the first attempts to make programming easier by moving away from numerical codes

1952 May
IBM announced their 701 computer: the company's first commercial stored-program computer, based on the IAS design

1953
Magnetic core memory installed on Whirlwind, leading to increased performance and reliability

1954
IBM began deliveries of its 650 computer. The 650 was

cheaper than the 701 and used a magnetic drum memory. It
became popular with businesses and universities

J.H. Laning and Neil Zierler developed an algebraic compiler
for the Whirlwind: the first high-level algebraic language for
computers

1955
First commercial core memories made available, for the ERA
1103A computer

1956
Beginning of the SAGE air-defense system, using a computer
built by IBM after a design based on the Whirlwind. The full
SAGE system was completed by 1963

Librascope introduced the LGP-30, a small, inexpensive general-purpose drum computer

Bendix G-15 delivered, another inexpensive drum-based
computer with very good performance

IBM delivered its model 704 computer: a large scientific
machine that handled floating point numbers and used core
memory

1957
Burroughs "Atlas Guidance" Computer used to control the
launch of the Atlas missile. It was one of the first computers
to use transistors

IBM introduced the "RAMAC" ("Random Access"), a memory device based on rotating disks

The FORTRAN prgramming language offered for IBM 704.
This language is still in wide use in the 1990s

1958
SAGE air-defense system operational on a limited basis. System allowed on-line access, in graphical form, to data transmitted to and processed by its computers

Commercial transistorized computers, including the UNI-
VAC Solid State 80 and the Philco S-2000, were introduced.
These inaugurated the so-called "Second Generation" of
electronic computers

Sylvania developed the "Fieldata" family of computers: a line
of machines differing in size that were capable of running the
same software

Jack Kilby of Texas Instruments conceived of the integrated
circuit and constructed a basic prototype

1959

Independently of Kilby, Robert Noyce of Fairchild Semiconductor invented a process that made it practical to manufacture integrated circuits. Noyce would eventually be regarded as the inspiration for "Silicon Valley," the region south of San Francisco where integrated circuit production and design would take place

IBM announced their 1401 computer: an inexpensive computer that proved very popular with businesses, and which began to compete seriously with existing punched-card equipment

RCA delivered its 501 computer. The programming language COBOL was supplied with it

General Electric entered the commercial computer market with its model 210

1959–60

The U.S. banking industry adopted MICR: "magnetic ink character recognition," which allowed machines to read the data printed on checks

1960

IBM introduced a transistorized version of its 709 computer, the 7090. It becomes the most popular large "mainframe" computer of the early 1960s

U.S. Department of Defense issued a requirement that all computers supplied to it must be capable of compiling the COBOL programming language

December: a program written in the COBOL programming language runs on two different computers from different vendors. Programming no longer must be done separately for each brand of computer

Control Data Corporation introduced its first computer, the CDC 1604, designed by Seymour Cray

Digital Equipment Corporation introduced its first computer, the PDP-1. On advice from the venture capital firm that financed the company, it did not call it a "computer" but a "Programmed Data Processor" instead

1962

SDS, a California company founded by Max Palevsky, introduced the SDS 910. This was the first commercial computer to use silicon transistors

Ferranti, Ltd. of England introduced the Atlas: a large computer with many features that would later become standard, including "virtual memory" and an operating system

QUOTRON, a computerized stock quotation system using a Control Data Corporation computer, introduced. It became popular with stockbrokers and signalled the end of the "ticker tape"

First Departments of "Computer Science" appeared at a few universities in the United States. Twenty years later Computer Science would become one of the most popular undergraduate majors

1963
ASCII (American Standard Code for Information Interchange) standard promulgated, specifying the pattern of 7 bits to represent letters, numbers, punctuation, and control signals in computers

Burroughs Corporation installed the first of their B-5000 computers, which employed some of the advanced features pioneered by the Ferranti Atlas

1964
Honeywell introduced the H-200: a successful competitor to the IBM 1401, with software that allowed it to "emulate," or act like, an IBM 1401

Control Data delivered the CDC 6600: the first modern "supercomputer"

April 7: IBM announced the System/360 family of compatible machines

RCA announced the Spectra series of computers, which could run the same software as IBM's 360 machines. The Spectra computers were the first commercial machines to use integrated circuits

Digital Equipment Corporation introduced the PDP-6, a large computer that, with its successor the PDP-10, was popular for research on Artificial Intelligence (AI) and time-sharing

The "Green Machine" calculator built

The BASIC programming language developed at Dartmouth

SABRE, an on-line computerized airline reservation system developed by American Airlines and IBM, becomes operational

1965
April: First shipment of the Digital Equipment Corporation PDP-8 minicomputer

Installations of the IBM System/360s began

First manned flights of the Gemini spacecraft

Minuteman ballistic missile systems operational

Internal Revenue Service began using Social Security Number as tax I.D. number

1966
NY Stock Exchange completed automation of its basic trading functions

1967
GE 635 system offered time-sharing as a commercial service

Shipments of semiconductor memory, as a replacement for magnetic core, began

IRS completed computerization of income tax processing, with a central facility in Martinsburg, West Virginia, and satellite locations around the United States

1968
October: the term "Software Engineering" coined at a NATO Conference, in response to the perception that computer programming had not kept up with advances in computer hardware

December: IBM agreed to "unbundle" its software: to charge separately for it and allow customers to purchase software from other suppliers. This action was the starting point for the commercial software industry

First manned Apollo flights, including Apollo 8, which circumnavigated the Moon on Christmas Eve

HP introduced the desk calculator HP 9100A

1969
Data General Nova minicomputer introduced. It was one of the first commercial machines to use medium-scale integrated circuits (MSI)

July: Neil Armstrong and Edwin Aldrin became the first human beings to walk on the moon. Their landing was almost canceled in the final seconds because of an overload of the Apollo Guidance Computer's memory, but on advice from Earth, they ignored the warnings and landed safely

ARPA-Net established, sponsored by the Defense Department's Advanced Research Projects Agency (ARPA). It eventually linked computers across the country, and laid the foundation for computer networking

The UNIX operating system developed at Bell Labs

1970
DEC introduced the PDP-11 minicomputer, which popularized the notion of a "bus," onto which a variety of additional circuit boards or peripheral products can be placed

IBM 370 series announced: an upgrade to the 360, using semiconductor memory in place of magnetic cores. IBM invented the floppy disk to store data that otherwise would be lost when power is switched off (that does not occur with core memory)

First automatic-teller machine installed

1971
Data General Super Nova became the first commercial computer actually delivered to use semiconductor memory

Intel 4004 microprocessor

1972
HP-35 pocket calculator

ILLIAC-IV installed at NASA. It had a parallel processing design that sought to break away from the model proposed in 1945 by von Neumann in his EDVAC report

Intel 8008 microprocessor

1972–74
Inexpensive calculators from Bowmar, among others, flooded the market

1973
May: Wang 2200 minicomputer introduced. With this product, Wang Laboratories shifted its focus to minicomputers from electronic calculators

Xerox Alto system, employing a bitmapped display, networking through Ethernet, and a mouse, developed

Universal Product Code—-the familiar bar code—-accepted by a grocer's trade association

1974
January: HP-65 programmable pocket calculator announced

Intel 8080 microprocessor announced; became the basis for the first personal computers

1975
January: MITS Altair computer kit announced in *Popular Electronics* article

1976
CRAY-1 supercomputer announced. Company was founded by Seymour Cray, who had left Control Data Corporation

IMSAI personal computer

1977
Summer: Apple II, TRS-80, Commodore Pet all announced and shown at a computer trade show

1978
Wang introduced their VS minicomputer system, which became one of the most popular office systems, and which inaugurated the concept of "office automation"

DEC VAX 11/780 announced

1979
HP-41C programmable pocket calculator

"Visicalc" introduced for Apple II. The first "spreadsheet" program, it was an immediate success and helped dispel the notion that the Apple was only a toy for hobbyists

1981
IBM introduced their personal computer, based on the Intel 8088 processor and using an operating system developed by Microsoft

Adam Osborne introduced his "portable" computer

1982
First SUN workstation announced

1983
Kaypro II, a portable patterned after the Osborne, introduced

TRS-80, Model 100, introduced the notion of a "laptop" computer

1984
Apple Macintosh introduced

1985
DEC Microvax II, a compact version of their popular VAX computer, introduced

1986
Burroughs and Sperry merged to form UNISYS, briefly becoming the second largest computer manufacturer

1987
Workstations employing RISC architecture announced by various companies

1988–1993
The pace of technical innovation and introduction of new products continues. Workstations, personal computers, networks, and notebook-sized machines characterize much of the innovation, while supercomputers move from the von Neumann architecture of single processors to massively parallel designs. Devices that combine computing and communications in a pocket size appear. Mainframe computers continue to be developed, although their dominance of the industry is eclipsed by networks of high-performance workstations and so-called "file servers"

Photographic Negative Numbers

The Smithsonian Institution offers the public the opportunity to purchase photographs which have been approved by curatorial units. For charges and information on ordering photographs, write: Photographic Services, NMAH-CB054, Smithsonian Institution, Washington, D.C. 20560.

	Negative Number	
Object	Black/White Print	Color Slide
Quipu	89-11875	89-11875
Counter	N89-095-14	N89-98
Chinese abacus	19876	89-13537
Japanese abacus	85-13312	85-13312
Russian abacus	79-10143	79-10143
John Napier	90-2837	none
Napier's rods	58996-C	89-13538
Slate	77304-D	92-6050
Circular interest table	80-16432	80-16432
Book of mathematical tables	92-4977	89-20455
Blaise Pascal	46835-B	none
Lepine's adding machine	72-9841	89-19705
Webb adder	86-10562	86-10562
Jacquard loom	77041	75-11368
Woven picture of J.M. Jacquard	P-61986	74-2458
Thomas arithmometer	P-651074-B	89-13225
Underside of a Thomas arithmometer	P-651074-A	none
Curta calculating machine	86-204	86-204
Schilt adding machine	58996	89-13539
Scheutz difference engine	74-11266	89-22028

Object	Black/White Print	Color Slide
Baldwin calculating machine	30943-A	89-13541
Odhner calculating machine	P-63181	none
Comptometer: macaroni box model	39034	89-13536
One of Felt's first eight Comptometers	82-5302	82-5302
Advertisement for a Comptometer, 1905	90-2314	90-2314
W.S. Burroughs adding machine	58996-G	89-13226
Ritty cash register	73-3169	73-3169
National cash register	89-12808	89-12808
Relay in the Morse telegraph system	46790-V	none
Hollerith tabulating system (overall)	79-10952	79-10952
IBM tabulating equipment	92-11982/22	92-11983
German Navy Enigma cipher machine	90-3649	90-3649
Bombe deciphering machine	90-3650	none
Section of a totalisator	91-6363	91-6362
Totalisator installation	90-740	none
Mark I computer (original installation)	74-7494	none
Control panel of the Bell Labs Model V	92-14370	92-14370
EDVAC computer component	61758-A	none
Transistors	61755	none
ENIAC computer at Moore School of Electrical Engineering	72-2644	none
ENIAC computer (view of portions)	90-7163/11	90-7165
IAS computer (former exhibit)	64771	86-14665
Whirlwind computer as installed at MIT	92-13335	none
UNIVAC I computer	71-2641	none
Grace Hopper and colleagues at the keyboard of a UNIVAC computer	83-14878	none
IBM S/360 computer	92-14060	none
PDP-8 minicomputer	90-5950	90-5950
Gemini digital computer	89-13133/6	89-21491
Minuteman missile, being launched	89-21493	89-21493
Minuteman guidance system	89-13133/2	89-21496
Apollo Guidance Computer	90-407	89-20456
Diagram of astronauts using the Apollo Guidance Computer to navigate	89-21490	89-21494
Microvax superminicomputer	92-4863	none
Electronic calculators		
Keyboard for the Green Machine	81-4598	81-4598
HP9100A programmable calculator	81-4603	81-4603
HP-35	83-8173	83-8173
Bowmar	89-11896	89-11896
TI SR-10	89-11897	89-11897
HP-41CV	88-11849-30	none
HP-41CV in space	92-14288	none
Intel 8080A microprocessor	92-7008-29	92-7010
Altair 8800 microcomputer	88-19284	88-19284
IMSAI microcomputer	92-13443	92-13443
TRS-80 microcomputer	92-13447	92-13447
Apple II microcomputer	91-14186	91-14186
IBM personal computer	92-7800	92-7800
Osborne computer	86-13443	86-13443
TRS-80 Model 100 microcomputer	91-692	none
Macintosh microcomputer	91-14187	91-14187
Xerox Alto workstation	90-2234	90-2234
Cray-1 computer on exhibit	92-15054/6	89-21494
SUN-2 workstation	91-14954	91-14954
SUN SPARC workstation	92-7086/6	none

Glossary

analog *adj* : of or relating to a device in which numerical values are represented by continuous physical quantities. A common example is a mechanical clock, which represents time by the continuous motion of the gears and hands. Compare to digital

artificial intelligence *n* : the simulation of human thinking by machines, especially computers

avionics *n* (from aviation electronics) : an electronic system associated with an aircraft, such as a system that manages flight navigation and communication — avionic *adj*

binary *adj* : of or relating to the number two. A binary system is characterized by two states such as on or off, yes or no, signal or no signal. Binary arithmetic is arithmetic that uses only two digits (zero and one) rather than the usual ten. In electronic computing, a high or low electrical signal represents a 1 or a 0

bit *n* (from binary digit) : a binary digit (one or zero), and hence the smallest unit of information in a computer

black box *n* 1 : any electronic system whose internal structure is of no concern to the user   2 : specifically, the colloquial name for a flight data recorder, a device that records details of an aircraft's control and performance so that the cause of a crash or other problem can be determined

bug *n* : a flaw in the instructions for or operation of a device. American engineers used the term from the late nineteenth century. As early as 1944, malfunctions in the ASCC Mark I computer were called bugs

bus *n* : a set of internal circuits that transmits data and control signals from one part of a computer to another. In some minicomputers and several early personal computers, the design of the bus was made public, making it easy to provide additional circuit boards

byte *n* : a group of bits used to encode a letter of the alphabet, a punctuation mark, and each of the other characters found on an ordinary typewriter. For many years, the standard byte has been eight bits

CAD *abbr* : computer-aided design

CAD/CAM *abbr* : computer-aided design/computer-assisted manufacturing

calculating machine *n* : a computing device that performs arithmetic by representing numbers by the motion of gears, wheels and other parts. The term sometimes refers to any such machine and is sometimes restricted to machines that multiply other than by repeated addition

calculator *n* 1 : a calculating machine   2 : in the late 1940s and early 1950s, an electromechanical or electronic computer   3 : an electronic computing device, often handheld, that performs the four arithmetic functions of addition, subtraction, multiplication, and division

central processing unit *n* : the section of a computer that performs arithmetic and carries out logical operations

chip *n* : microchip

COBOL *acr* : <u>co</u>mmon <u>b</u>usiness-<u>o</u>riented <u>l</u>anguage, a computer language developed in the late 1950s for business users. Through a directive by the U.S. Defense Department that required its availability on all DoD computers, COBOL was developed to a point where the same program would run correctly on machines supplied by different manufacturers—a revolutionary achievement at the time—hence the term "common."

compiler *n* : a computer program that translates instructions written in a programming language into the codes (usually long strings of binary numbers) that a computer uses internally

computer *n* 1 : from the seventeenth century to the mid-1950s, a person who performed calculations, especially for astronomers and scientists who handled large amounts of numerical data   2 : from 1945 to about 1955, a machine that could be instructed to perform a sequence of calculations automatically and store and retrieve intermediate results   3 : at present, an electronic device that can process, transmit, store, retrieve and otherwise handle coded information (as numbers, text, graphics and internally stored programs) in a general and flexible way as directed by the programs

computer graphics *n* : charts, drawings, and other images created and manipulated by computer technology

console *n* : the primary control section of a large computer. It usually resembles a desk into which are mounted computer keyboards, displays, switches, and other electronic equipment

control *n* : the part of a computer or calculator that directs other functions such as performing arithmetic, storing or retrieving numbers from memory, or sending data to a printer

core *n* : a computer memory that uses a grid of doughnut-shaped pieces of magnetic material. Each of these pieces may be magnetized in either of two directions to store a bit of information

counter *n* 1 : an object such as a bead or pebble used to represent a number in an abacus   2 : a device that records numbers that increase or decrease by a fixed increment. For example, the odometer on a car is a counter, increasing by units of 1/10 of a mile (compare to register).

cpu *abbr* : central processing unit

data *n* (from the Latin for "things which are given") : information fed in a form that can be used

database *n* : an ordered collection of numerical or textual information. Examples range from a list of names and addresses to a table of numbers describing the interaction of two molecules in a chemical reaction

data processing *n* : the conversion of information into a more useful form

debug *v* : to correct a bug

digital *adj* (from the Latin *digitus*, finger) : representing data by discrete units. Compare to analog

digitize *v* : to convert information into strings of numbers, especially binary numbers (ones and zeros)

DIP *acr* : Dual In-line Package. The way that most integrated circuits have been packaged. A silicon chip itself is typically smaller than a fingernail. To become part of a computer it must have leads attached to it and be enclosed in a rugged casing that protects it from damage. Most commonly it is encased in black plastic, with two rows of parallel leads down either side, like a centipede. As computer manufacturers strive for ever-smaller packaging, these are giving way to single in-line packaging.

electromechanical *adj* 1 : of or relating to a calculating machine that is electrically powered but represents numbers by the position of its parts   2 : of or relating to a device in which numbers are represented by electrical signals, while the switching and transfer of data is done by devices with moving parts such as relays of rotary switches. The second definition is used in this book

electronic *adj* : involving the movement of electrons through a gas, vacuum, or semiconductor

hardware *n* : the electronic and mechanical portions of a computer (compare to software)

human factor *n* : an aspect of design relating to the way people use a machine. Human factors include the placement and shape of instruments, control pedals, and knobs; the layout, colors, and brightness of computer screens; and the design of instructions for users of a program

IC *abbr* : integrated circuit, *q.v.*

inertial guidance *n* : control of an aircraft from precision measurements of acceleration, using self-contained automatic instruments that continuously calculate and adjust for variables in flight

integrated circuit *n* : a circuit in which the functions of several distinct electronic components (as resistors, transistors, and capacitors) are performed by a small unit of suitably treated semiconducting material. Integrated circuits frequently contain the equivalent of relays and vacuum tubes, arranged so that they can represent numbers digitally

K *abbr* : kilobyte or kilobytes (e.g., 24K = 24 x 1024 = 24,576 bytes)

kilobyte *n* : one thousand twenty-four bytes. The number 1024 equals two to the tenth power

language *see* programming language

mainframe *n* 1 : the central part of a large computer, including the central processing unit   2 : colloquially, in recent years, a large computer (compare to minicomputer and microcomputer)

megabyte *n* 1 : two to the twentieth power, or 1,048,576, bytes 2 : a million bytes

memory *n* : the section of a computer which records data for later use or recall

microchip *n* : a small piece of semiconducting material containing one or more integrated circuits

microcomputer *n* : a small computer, usually intended for only one user, that carries out data processing using integrated circuits

microprocessor *n* : a microchip that can be programmed to function in more than one way. Microprocessors were first designed for electronic calculators and then used as central elements of microcomputers

minicomputer *n* : a moderate-sized, and once relatively inexpensive, digital computer, often applied to a special purpose such as data reduction in a laboratory or process control in industry, and well suited to interactive use. The name became common in the late 1960s. Compare to mainframe and microcomputer

network *n* : a group of computers electronically linked to exchange data and software

OEM *abbr* : original equipment manufacturer

operating system *n* : a program or set of programs that manages the operation of a computer and its peripherals

parallel *adj* 1 : of or relating to a method of calculation in which all the digits of a number are processed at the same time (as in an adding machine, at the turn of a crank)   2 : of or relating to a computer design in which the digits of a word are processed simultaneously and in which more than one set of instructions is executed on the data at the same time (compare to serial)   3 : of or relating to a type of computer that has many processors, each of which operates somewhat independently on different parts of the data

peripheral *n*: any of a number of devices, such as card readers, printers, plotters, and monitors, attached to the central processing unit of a computer

personal computer *n*: a computer used by a single individual. Most personal computers are microcomputers, although a few earlier computers were sometimes used as personal computers

program *n*: a set of instructions that directs a computer to solve a problem or perform an operation. Often these instructions are given in a programming language

programming language *n*: a set of terms for instructing a computer, with rules for their use. Since the terms and associated rules have a syntax and semantics, they are called a language

real-time *adj*: of or relating to a device that collects, analyzes or acts upon information about events as quickly as they occur

reduced instruction set computer *n*: a computer that uses a small set of simple, rapidly executable instructions, designed to operate more rapidly than computers with more sophisticated instructions that take more time to execute. Such computers have become increasingly common since 1985

register *n* 1 : a book or other device for recording data (e.g., the cash register, a machine that records transactions in a store)   2 : in a calculating machine, a mechanism such as a set of number wheels that stores or displays numbers entered or results of computations 3 : in a computer or electronic calculator, a location in the memory with small capacity but short access time. It may be used for a designated purpose. Numbers stored in a register need not be altered by a fixed increment (compare to counter)

RISC *acr* 1 : reduced instruction set computer   2 : of or relating to such a computer

robot *n*: a computer system that can be programmed to interact with its physical surroundings without immediate human assistance; especially one guided by automatic controls

semiconducting *adj*: of, relating to, or having the properties of a semiconductor

semiconductor *n*: a material (as silicon) that conducts electrons in some circumstances but not others. The conductivity of a semiconductor is often altered by introducing impurities into its crystalline structure

serial *adj* 1 : of or relating to a computing device in which the digits of a number are processed one at a time. People doing arithmetic with a pencil and paper typically add or multiply serially, starting from the right   2 : of or relating to a computing device in which instructions are executed one at a time. Compare to parallel

software *n* : any or all computer programs, including not only those that solve a problem or do a job for a particular user (applications software), but also compilers and operating systems

SPARC *acr* : scalable processor architecture. A design of computers that uses a relatively small number of instructions. The term was introduced by SUN Microsystems, Inc., in about 1987–1988. "Scalable" refers to SUN's claim that the design lends itself to a variety of implementations, from simple desktop personal computers to large networked systems.

supercomputer *n* : a computer designed expressly for the rapid calculation of data. Supercomputers are used to study problems of fluid dynamics, astrophysics, and molecular biology, and by military agencies involved with weapons design and cryptography

transistor *n* : an electronic component in which the functions of a vacuum tube are carried out by appropriately treated sections of semiconducting material. Transistors were widely used in computer circuits in the 1960s

vacuum tube *n* : an evacuated tube in which electrical voltages are used to control the flow of electrons emitted by a filament and attracted to a positively charged plate. Vacuum tubes are used to amplify electrical signals and served as electronic switches in computers of the 1940s and 1950s

word *n* : a set of bits that occupies one storage location in a computer and is processed as a unit by computer circuits

word length *n* : the number of bits in a word. A typical personal computer has a word length of 16 or 32 bits

workstation *n* : a computer terminal with sophisticated graphics, networking and calculating abilities. Workstations may be small, separate computers or parts of a large computer system

Bibliography

l'Académie royale des sciences. 1735. Machine arithmétique, inventée par M. Lepine. *Recueil des Machines approuvées par l'Académie royale des sciences* 4:131–136.

Adrosko, Rita. 1982. The invention of the Jacquard mechanism. *Bulletin de liaison du centre international d'étude des textiles anciens* 55–56:89–113.

Aiken, Howard H. 1937. Proposed automatic calculating machine. Reprinted in *The Origins of Digital Computers Selected Papers*, comp. Brian Randell, 1982, pp. 195–201. New York: Springer-Verlag.

Aly, Goetz, and Karl H. Roth. 1984. *Die restlose Erfassung: Volkszaehlen, Identifizieren, Aussondern im Nationalsozialismus.* Berlin: Rotbuch Verlag.

Anderson, Charnel. 1962. *Technology in American Education 1650–1900.* Bulletin of the Office of Education of the U.S. Department of Health, Education, and Welfare, No. 19.

Andrew, Christopher, ed. 1986. *Codebreaking and Signals Intelligence.* London: Frank Cass.

Anonymous. 1890. The Census of the United States. *Scientific American* August 30, cover and p. 132.

Anonymous. 1931. *The Totalisator.* Baltimore: The Automatic Calculating Machine Company of Maryland.

Anonymous. 1939. William Seward Burroughs. *National Cyclopaedia of American Biography* 27:383–384. New York: James T. White & Co.

Anonymous. 1953. *A Survey of Automatic Digital Computers.* Washington, D.C.: Office of Naval Research.

Anonymous. 1955. Dorr Eugene Felt. *National Cyclopaedia of American Biography*, 40:23–24. New York: James T. White & Co.

Anonymous. 1985. *Understanding Computers: Computer Basics.* Alexandria, Va.: Time-Life Books.

Anonymous. 1986. *Understanding Computers: Input/Output.* Alexandria Va.: Time-Life Books.

Anonymous. 1988. Ein grosser Erfinder ist nicht mehr unter uns. *Historische Buerowelt* November 36:26.

Archibald, R.C. 1948. *Mathematical Table Makers.* New York: Scripta Mathematica.

Ascher, Marcia, and Robert Ascher. 1978. *Code of the Quipu Databook.* Ann Arbor: University of Michigan Press.

Ascher, Marcia, and Robert Ascher. 1981. *Code of the Quipu: A Study in Media, Mathematics, and Culture.* Ann Arbor: University of Michigan Press.

Aspray, William, ed. 1990. *Computing before Computers.* Ames: Iowa State University Press.

Aspray, William. 1991. *John von Neumann and the Origins of Modern Computing.* Cambridge, Mass.: MIT Press.

Augarten, Stan. 1984. *Bit by Bit: An Illustrated History of Computers.* New York: Ticknor & Fields.

Austrian, Geoffrey D. 1982. *Herman Hollerith: Forgotten Giant of Information Processing.* New York: Columbia University Press.

Baillie, C.H. 1982. *Watchmakers and Clockmakers of the World,* vol. 1. London: N.A.G. Press.

Barnard, F.P. 1916. *The Casting-Counter and the Counting-Board.* Oxford: Oxford University Press.

Beauclair, W. de. 1968. *Rechnen mit Maschinen: Eine Bildgeschichte der Rechentechnik.* Braunschweig: Friedr. Vieweg & Sohn.

Bedini, Silvio A. 1972. *The Life of Benjamin Banneker.* New York: Scribners.

Bell, C. Gordon, J. Craig Mudge, and John E. McNamara. 1978. *Computer Engineering: A DEC View of Hardware Systems Design.* Bedford, Mass.: Digital Press.

Bell, C. Gordon, and Allen Newell. 1971. *Computer Structures: Readings and Examples.* New York: McGraw-Hill.

Bernstein, Mark. 1989. John Patterson rang up success with the Incorruptible Cashier. *Smithsonian* 20(3):150–154.

Bigelow, Julian. 1980. Computer Development at the Institute for Advanced Study. *A History of Computing in the Twentieth Century, A Collection of Essays,* ed. N. Metropolis, J. Howlett, and Gian-Carlo Rota, pp. 291–310. New York: Academic Press.

Braun, Ernest, and Stuart Macdonald. 1982. *Revolution in Minature: The History and Impact of Semiconductor Electronics.* Cambridge: Cambridge University Press.

Bryden, D.J. 1992. *Napier's Bones: A History and Instruction Manual.* London: Harriet Wynter Ltd.

Buck, Fred S. [1945.] *Horse Race Betting: A Complete Account of Pari-Mutuel and Bookmaking Operations.* New York: Greenberg.

Ceruzzi, Paul. 1983. *Reckoners: The Prehistory of the Digital Computer, from Relays to the Stored Program Concept, 1935–1945.* Westport, Conn.: Greenwood Press.

Ceruzzi, Paul. 1989. *Beyond the Limits: Flight Enters the Computer Age.* Cambridge, Mass.: MIT Press.

Cohen, I. Bernard. 1992. Howard H. Aiken, Harvard University, and IBM: Cooperation and Conflict. *Science at Harvard University: Historical Perspectives,* ed. C.A. Elliott and M.W. Rossiter, pp. 251–284. Bethlehem, Pa.: Lehigh University Press.

Cohen, Patricia C. 1982. *A Calculating People: The Spread of Numer-*

acy in Early America. Chicago: University of Chicago Press.

Comrie, Leslie J. 1933. *The Hollerith and Powers Tabulating Machines*. London: Office Machine Users' Association.

Connolly, J. ca. 1967. *History of Computing in Europe*. [np]: IBM World Trade Corporation.

Croarken, Mary. 1990. *Early Scientific Computing in Britain*. Oxford: Clarendon Press.

Darby, Edwin. 1968. *It All Adds Up: The Growth of the Victor Comptometer Corporation*. [np]: Victor Comptometer Corporation.

Evans, Bob O. 1986. System/360: A Retrospective View. *Annals of the History of Computing* 8:155–179.

Everett, Robert R. 1980. Whirlwind. *A History of Computing in_the Twentieth Century, A Collection of Essays*, ed. N. Metropolis, J. Howlett, and Gian-Carlo Rota, pp. 365–384. New York: Academic Press.

Freiberger, Paul, and Michael Swaine. 1984. *Fire in the Valley: The Making of the Personal Computer*. Berkeley: Osborne/McGraw-Hill.

Glaisher, J.W.L. 1911. Table, Mathematical. *Encyclopaedia Britannica* 26:325–336. Cambridge: Cambridge University Press.

Goldberg, Adele, ed. 1988. *A History of Personal Workstations*. New York: ACM Press.

Goldstine, Herman H. 1972. *The Computer from Pascal to von Neumann*. Princeton: Princeton University Press.

Gupta, A., and H.D. Toong, eds. 1985. *Insights into Personal Computers*. New York: IEEE Press.

Hall, Eldon. 1982. The Apollo Guidance Computer: a Designer's View. *Computer Museum Report* Fall, 2–5.

Hall, Mark, and John Barry. 1990. *Sunburst: the Ascent of Sun Microsystems*. Chicago: Contemporary Books.

Herzstark, Curt. 1987. Interview with Erwin Tomash, September 10 and 11, 1987. Oral History 140. Charles Babbage Institute, Minneapolis, Minnesota.

Hodges, Andrew. 1983. *Alan Turing: The Enigma*. New York: Simon & Schuster.

Holman, Alfred L. 1921. *A Register of the Ancestors of Dorr E. Felt and Agnes (McNulty) Felt*. Chicago: for Dorr E. Felt.

Horsburgh, E.M., ed. 1914. *Modern Instruments and Methods of Calculation: A Handbook of the Napier Tercentenary Exhibition*. London: G. Bell and Sons, Ltd., and the Royal Society of Edinburgh. Republished by Tomash Publishers in Los Angeles, California, in 1982.

House, Chuck. 1988. Hewlett-Packard and Personal Computing Systems. In *A History of Personal Workstations*, Adele Goldberg, ed. New York: ACM Press.

Hudson, J. Paul. 1979. Brass Casting Counters (or Jettons) Found at Jamestown. *Quarterly Bulletin Archeological Society of Virginia* 34:112–113.

Hurd, Cuthbert C. 1981. Early IBM Computers: Edited Testimony.

Annals of the History of Computing 3:163–182.

Jarett, Keith. 1984. HP-41 in Orbit. *Professional Computing* Oct/Nov: 50–54.

Johnson, J., et al. 1989. The Xerox Star: A Retrospective. *Computer* 22(9):11–28.

Kahn, David. 1967. *The Codebreakers: The Story of Secret Writing.* New York: Macmillan.

Kahn, David. 1991. *Seizing the Enigma: The Race to Break the German U-Boat Codes, 1939–1943.* Boston: Houghton Mifflin Company.

Kenney, Donald P. 1978. *Minicomputers: Low-Cost Computer Power for Management.* New York: AMACOM.

Kidwell, Peggy A. 1986. The Webb Adder. *Rittenhouse* 1:12–18.

Kozaczuk, Wladyslaw. 1984. *Enigma: How the German Cipher Was Broken and How It Was Read by the Allies in World War II,* trans. C. Kasparek. [Frederick, Md.]: University Publications of America, Inc.

Kruh, Louis. 1985. An Armchair View of the Smithsonian Institution Cipher Machine Exhibit. *Cryptologia* 9:38–51.

Lammers, Susan, ed. 1989. *Programmers at Work.* Redmond, Wash.: Microsoft Press.

Lavington, Simon. 1980. *Early British Computers.* Bedford, Mass.: Digital Press.

Levering, Robert, M. Katz, and M. Moskowitz. 1984. *The Computer Entrepreneurs.* New York: New American Library.

Lewin, Ronald. 1978. *Ultra Goes to War: The First Account of World War II's Greatest Secret Based on Official Documents.* New York: McGraw-Hill.

Liebowitz, Burt H., and Richard S. Wolf. 1973. The Use of Minicomputers in Racetrack Totalisator Systems. *Proceedings of the IEEE* 61:1626–1633.

Lindgren, Michael. 1987. *Glory and Failure: The Difference Engines of Johann Mueller, Charles Babbage and Georg and Edvard Scheutz,* trans. Craig G. McKay. Linkoping, Sweden: Linkoping University. Reprinted by MIT Press in 1990.

Linvill, John G., and C. Lester Hogan. 1977. Intellectual and Economic Fuel for the Electronics Revolution. *Science* 195:1107–1113.

Locke, L. Leland. 1922. Frank Stephen Baldwin, Founder of Mechanical Arithmetic. *Typewriter Topics* June: 109–111.

Locke, L. Leland. 1923. *The Ancient Quipu or Peruvian Knot Record.* [New York]: The American Museum of Natural History.

Locke, L. Leland. 1928. Frank Stephen Baldwin. *Dictionary of American Biography,* 1:533. New York: Charles Scribners.

Loughlin, G.F. 1918. *Slate in 1917.* Washington, D.C.: Government Printing Office.

Lukoff, Herman. 1979. *From Dits to Bits: A Personal History of the Electronic Computer*. Portland, Oreg.: Robotics Press.

Marcosson, Isaac Frederick. 1945. *Whenever Men Trade: The Romance of the Cash Register*. New York: Dodd, Mead & Co. Reprinted by Arno Press of New York in 1972.

Martin, Ernst. 1925. *Die Rechenmaschinen und ihre Entwicklungsgeschichte*. Pappenheim: J. Meyer. An English translation, edited by Peggy A. Kidwell and Michael R. Williams, was published by MIT Press in 1992.

Martin, T.C. 1891. Counting a Nation by Electricity. *The Electrical Engineer* 12(184):521–530.

Menninger, Karl. 1969. *Number Words and Number Symbols. A Cultural History of Numbers*, trans. Paul Broneer. Cambridge, Mass.: MIT Press.

Merzbach, Uta C. 1977. *Georg Scheutz and the First Printing Calculator*. Washington, D.C.: Smithsonian Institution Press.

Mims, Forrest M. III. 1985. *Siliconnections: Coming of Age in the Electronic Era*. New York: McGraw-Hill Book Company.

Mitchiner, Michael. 1988. *Jetons, Medalets & Tokens, the Medieval Period and Nuremberg*, vol. 1. London: Seaby.

Napier, John. 1990. *Rabdology*, translated by W.F. Richardson, introduction by Robin E. Rider. Cambridge, Mass.: MIT Press. Translation of the Latin edition of 1617.

Needham, Joseph, with the collaboration of Wang Ling. 1959. *Science and Civilization in China*, vol. 3. Cambridge: Cambridge University Press.

Neugebauer, O. 1975. *A History of Ancient Mathematical Astronomy*, vol. 1. New York: Springer-Verlag.

Norberg, Arthur. 1990. High-Technology Calculation in the Early 20th Century: Punched Card Machinery in Business and Government. *Technology and Culture* 31:753–779.

Noyce, Robert N., and Marcian E. Hoff, Jr. 1981. A History of Microprocessor Development at Intel. *IEEE Micro* 1(1): 8–22.

d'Ocagne, Maurice. 1986. *Le Calcul Simplifie: Graphical and Mechanical Methods for Simplifying Calculation*, trans. J. Howlett and M.R. Williams. Cambridge, Mass.: MIT Press. The original French version of this book was published by Gauthier-Villars in Paris in 1894, with later editions in 1905 and 1928.

Osborne, Adam, and John Dvorak. 1984. *Hypergrowth: the Rise and Fall of Osborne Computer Corporation*. Berkeley, Calf.: Idthekkethan Books.

Patterson, David A. 1985. Reduced Instruction Set Computers. *Communications of the ACM* 28:8–21.

Posselt, E.A. 1988. *The Jacquard Machine Analyzed and Explained*. Philadelphia: under the auspices of the Pennsylvania Museum and School of Industrial Art.

Prescott, G.B. 1860. *History, Theory and Practice of the Electric Telegraph*. Boston: Ticknor and Fields.

Pugh, E.W., L.R. Johnson, and J.H. Palmer. 1991. *IBM's 360 and Early 370 Systems.* Cambridge, Mass.: MIT Press.

Pullan, J.M. 1970. *The History of the Abacus.* New York: Praeger.

Putney, Diane T., ed. 1987. *ULTRA and the Army Air Forces in World War II.* Washington, D.C.: Office of Air Force History.

Redmond, Kent C., and Thomas M. Smith. 1980. *Project Whirlwind: The History of a Pioneer Computer.* Bedford, Mass.: Digital Press.

Reid-Green, Keith S. 1989. The History of Census Tabulation. *Scientific American* 260(2):98–103.

Rifkin, Glenn, and George Harrar. 1988. *The Ultimate Entrepreneur: The Story of Ken Olsen and Digital Equipment Corporation.* Chicago: Contemporary Books.

Roberts, H. Edward, and William Yates. 1975. Exclusive! Altair 8800 The most powerful minicomputer project ever presented—can be built for under $400. *Popular Electronics* 7(1):33–38.

Rose, Frank. 1989. *West of Eden: The End of Innocence at Apple Computer.* New York: Penguin.

Siewiorek, Daniel C., C.G. Bell, and A. Newell, eds. 1982. *Computer Structures: Principles and Examples.* New York: McGraw-Hill.

Snow, Richard F. 1990. Carpets in the Cards. *Invention & Technology* 6(2):5.

Stern, Nancy. 1981. *From ENIAC to UNIVAC, An Appraisal of Eckert-Mauchly Computers.* Bedford, Mass.: Digital Press.

Tomayko, James E. 1987. Computers in Spaceflight: the NASA Experience. *Encyclopedia of Computer Science and Technology* 18: supplement 3. New York: Marcel Dekker.

Truesdell, L. 1965. *The Development of Punch Card Tabulation in the Bureau of the Census 1890–1940.* Washington, D.C.: Government Printing Office.

Turck, J.A.V. 1921. *Origin of Modern Calculating Machines.* Chicago: under the auspices of the Western Society of Engineers.

Voelker, John. 1988. The PDP-8. *IEEE Spectrum* 25(11):86–92.

Walford, C. 1871. Calculating Machines. In *The Insurance Cyclopaedia* 1:411–412. London: C. & E. Layton.

Walker, Virginia C. 1981. Blueprint for Success—Pioneer Day 1981. *Annals of the History of Computing* 3:400–407.

Warren, Jim. 1977. Personal and hobby computing: an overview. *Computer* 10(3):10–15.

Willcox, Walter F. 1944. Herman Hollerith. *Dictionary of American Biography,* 21:415–416. New York: Charles Scribners.

Williams, Michael R. 1985. *A History of Computing Technology.* Englewood Cliffs, N.J.: Prentice-Hall.

Yoshino, Yozo. 1963. *The Japanese Abacus Explained,* with an introduction by Martin Gardner. New York: Dover.

Index